Of Mountains and Men

An Extraordinary Journey to Explore why Some People
Feel the Irresistible Urge to Climb Mountains

Mateo Cabello

GW00750980

Oxford Alpine Club

Oxford Alpine Club Books
www.oxfordalpineclub.co.uk

First published in the UK by the Oxford Alpine Club, 2016

ISBN 978-0-9567288-9-0

To Donald, David and Brigid

To Prabhass,
with gratitude,
in the hope you will
love the book

Mateo

Contents

Left: The Matterhorn. The Hörnli Ridge, attempted by William, Ian and James in 1948, runs up the centre of the picture, with the steep North Face to the right.

Foreword

by Stephen Venables

I was just twenty-four when I first saw the bronze plaque in Zermatt's churchyard marking the grave of William Bell, Ian McKean and James Ogilvie – 'friends from Oxford who died together on the Matterhorn'. I was alone in Zermatt, waiting for a spell of settled weather to attempt a solo ascent of the Matterhorn's north face. Eking out my dwindling fund of Swiss francs at the Bahnhof dormitory, watching the weather forecast each day, going for walks to kill time, brooding over my inner turmoil, torn between ambition and foreboding, I was in an impressionable state which made the memorial inscription almost unbearably poignant. However, it wasn't just the stark reminder that I too could end up buried in this graveyard, which struck me: there were other, deeper, resonances.

It was only three years since I too had graduated from Oxford. During my final summer, three contemporaries from the Oxford University Mountaineering Club had also been killed in an alpine accident. They had died on Mont Blanc, but one of them had been my partner two years before that, in 1973, when I first climbed the Matterhorn by the Hörnli Ridge – the same ridge where Bell, McKean and Ogilvie died in 1948. So there was a sad familiarity with youthful optimism snuffed out, lives unlived, families damaged. There was also a particular personal connection, because James Ogilvie was my father's first cousin.

Their grandfather – my great-grandfather, William Ogilvie – did several climbs around Zermatt in 1872, including what must have been one of the very first ascents of the Weisshorn. He wanted to climb the Matterhorn too but it was only seven years since the first ascent had been marred by a fatal accident, so his mother refused to allow him on the mountain. How prescient, you might conclude. And how ironic that the grandson should die on the very same mountain. However, the reality is that for all its hyped melodrama, the Matterhorn by its normal Hörnli Ridge is not a particularly hard or dangerous climb: the Weisshorn is actually a harder peak. A careless slip or momentary loss of concentration – or sheer bad luck – can happen anywhere. All we can do is mourn with that other mother – James's mother – the loss of her son.

A few days after that melancholic afternoon in the graveyard in May 1978, I did finally set foot on the North Face but after getting about a thousand feet up the still wintry wall, terrified by the vicious winds blasting the peak, I retreated, suitably chastened. About a year later I returned briefly to Oxford and ended up sharing a house with James Ogilvie's nephew. (He is also called James and recently climbed Mount Vinson in Antarctica, keeping the Ogilvie mountain tradition alive). By chance we were living next door to his grandmother, my great Aunt Mary, mother of the James who died in 1948. Now an old lady, retired after a lifetime as a distinguished champion of women's education, she was a wonderful person, always interested in what we were up to and generous in sharing memories of her own life and family, including her lost son. No-one ever 'gets over' the loss of a child. The sadness was still there to see. But so was the pride and joy, as she brought out the four-decades-old letters and diaries.

I wish I had paid closer attention at the time. As the years passed, all I could recall were vague memories of words written by a young officer serving in India that seemed remarkably mature yet full of youthful idealism. So I was delighted when I heard recently that Mateo Cabello was researching a book, not just about James Ogilvie, but about all three of the young men who died on that July day now almost seven decades ago. Like me, Mateo came across the grave just after completing the Haute Route from Chamonix to Zermatt (he on foot; I on ski). He too was moved by the simple inscription – so moved that, as he relates, it inspired in him a determination to find out more about these three young men. What followed was a remarkable detective story, enhanced by the kind of serendipitous connections the Internet has made possible, as he built up a picture of the three Oxford friends.

Right from the start, Mateo Cabello was clear that he was not trying to find exactly what happened on 25th July 1948: he was not in the ghoulish business of trying to reconstruct an accident. How or why they fell was irrelevant. Far more important to him was the realisation that all three had been at Oxford immediately after serving in the Second World War. They belonged to a generation which had made sacrifices and which was now building what many hoped would be a better world. Each, in his different way, was an idealist. Already by their early twenties they had achieved a lot, and, but for that unlucky accident, they might have gone on to do great things. How that accident happened – and whether it happened on the way up or on the way back from the summit – is not important.

I can't help being reminded of Ruth Mallory, whose husband died on Everest in 1924, writing to their mutual friend Geoffrey Winthrop Young, "I don't think I do feel that his death makes me the least more proud of him; it is his life that I loved and love. I know so absolutely that he could not have failed in courage or self-sacrifice. Whether he got to the top of the mountain or did not, whether he lived or died, makes no difference to my admiration for him". So too with these three men who perished on an equally famous, if easier, mountain. This book is a celebration of the lives they lived.

Stephen Venables is a former president of the Alpine Club, and the first Briton to climb Everest without supplementary oxygen.

Preface

Mountains are cathedrals: grand and pure,
the houses of my religion.
Anatoli Boukreev

I have a very deep love of mountains, but the idea of climbing one never crossed my mind. In essence, I am just a rambler: a hill-walker who is particularly fond of wandering in the Alps every summer, when my wife and I get the boots out of the wardrobe and head for Switzerland, Italy or France. We usually spend a fortnight there, walking eight to ten hours per day, away from smart phones, the Internet and the other burdens of modern life. During these trips, all we need is a light rucksack with a few essentials (food, water and a change of clothes), a hot shower at the end of the day, and basic accommodation for the night. The circular Tour of Mont Blanc, the Haute Route (which links Chamonix and Zermatt) and the Alpine Pass Route in the Bernese Oberland make up some of our favourite treks.

Despite such slim mountaineering credentials, I have spent the last three years on a quest to find out why some people feel the irresistible urge to climb mountains, sometimes even at the expense of their lives.

This question is neither new nor original, I admit. In fact, it has often been asked since climbing became popular around the mid-nineteenth century. In the aftermath of the Matterhorn disaster in 1865, when four climbers died after reaching its summit for the first time, *The Times* proclaimed its bewilderment: "Is it life? Is it duty? Is it common sense? Is it allowable? Is it wrong?" Derisive expressions such as 'acts of mock-heroism' or 'self-justification of the maladjusted' have been used to describe what pushes climbers to the heights. In 1937, the Swiss newspaper *Sport* went further when writing about those camping at the foot of the north face of the Eiger, waiting for a window of good weather to attempt climbing it, by calling them 'ludicrous earthworms'.

Even today the most seasoned climbers find it difficult to explain the attraction that mountains hold for them. This is especially remarkable considering that, as the mountaineer and author Joe Simpson describes, "What you stand to lose far outweighs whatever you could possibly win." In fact, dozens of people die every year in mountain-related accidents all over the world. Most of these are weekend aficionados. However, death makes no distinction and among those who die there are star climbers too, such as Alexey Bolotov, who was killed in May 2013 while trying an alternative approach to the Western Cwm, not far from the Lhotse face of Everest. Despite being well aware of the risks that climbing entails, those gripped by the 'climbing virus' cannot help but dream about their next adventure, their next expedition beyond the frontiers of the possible. Why? After all, as Robert Macfarlane explains in *Mountains of the Mind*, "Mountaineering isn't destiny – it doesn't have to happen to a person."

Finding an answer to that question without any personal climbing experience was a huge challenge. I have no idea what it is like to be hanging from a rope on an ice pillar as an avalanche hisses past me; neither have I gone through the agony of spending days tent-bound, high on a mountain, waiting for a storm to clear in order to descend it safely. I have never been in a situation where I have had to put my life in the hands of fellow climbers. What goes through your mind when passing below a big, trembling column of ice, as high as a ten-storey building, or trekking on a ridge cloaked with rotten snow where a single misstep could result in a fall of hundreds of feet onto a glacier? I honestly don't know.

In an attempt to fill this void, I have read as much as possible about other people's experiences in the mountains, including classic accounts about the first ascents in the Alps, such as Sir Leslie Stephen's *The Playground of Europe*, and Edward Whymper's *Scrambles Amongst the Alps*, as well as more recent tales of astonishing resilience against all the odds: books such as *K2, The Savage Mountain* by Charles Houston and Robert Bates, or *Annapurna* by Maurice Herzog. There have been books about death and hardship on distant peaks, such as Joe Simpson's *Dark Shadows Falling* and *Into Thin Air* by Jon Krakauer. However, there have also been inspirational stories about the triumph of the human spirit, some of the best being *No Picnic on Mount Kenya*, by Felice Benuzzi and *Freedom Climbers* by Bernadette McDonald. I enjoyed enormously reading what the protagonists of the most incredible climbing feats remembered about their exploits – recollections such as those of Walter Bonatti in *The Mountains of my Life* or Sir Edmund Hillary in *High Adventure*. In addition, I have read what those spouses who were left behind say about the long absences and, unfortunately, at times, the deaths of their loved ones, as in *Where the Mountain Casts its Shadow* by Maria Coffey. I have also watched documentaries such as *The Eiger: Wall of Death*, *Beyond Gravity* and *Pure Life*. Above all, I have had in-depth, inspiring conversations with climbers and mountaineers about their deeds, fears and motivation.

In hindsight, perhaps the lack of climbing experience has played in my favour as it is often said that in order to gain an objective, dispassionate perspective on a complex issue the best strategy is to distance yourself from the subject of your study. As a non-climber, I hope that I will be able to explain, in a manner that resonates with other non-climbers, why some people are so compelled to climb mountains. This was my purpose in writing this book. With enormous passion for the mountains, but also with the unbiased vision of an outsider, I started a personal journey to discover why for some people climbing is not just the embodiment of everything that is good and desirable in life, but can also become an ill-fated craving.

13

Three young students from Oxford – William Bell, Ian McKean and James Ogilvie – accompanied me throughout this adventure. I met them in a fortuitous way in a graveyard at the foot of the Matterhorn, where they had been buried after being killed in a climbing accident in 1948. I didn't know anything about them except what was written on the tombstone. Yet, without exactly knowing why, I felt compelled to learn more about their lives, dreams and aspirations. Back home I gradually unravelled their stories, and in doing so I found what I was looking for – the reason why for some people climbing mountains is a search for their own soul.

1. The Mountaineers' Cemetery in Zermatt

They shall grow not old, as we that are left grow old.
Robert Laurence Binyon

The view from Twära, in the Swiss Valais, is one of my favourite in the Alps. Located almost 4,000 feet above the village of St Niklaus, on a clear day there is a breath-taking 360-degree vista that includes some of the most stunning mountains in the world. In the north are the formidable walls of the Bernese Alps; to the east the Ticino Alps glimmer in the distance; to the south-west, the summits of the Weisshorn, the Zinalrothorn and the Dent Blanche surface like sea-foam amid a blue, stormy ocean of mountains. Right in front of you, the Dom (14,911 feet) rises majestically above the Hohberg glacier, so close that you could almost reach out and touch it.

The Dom is the highest peak in the Mischabel: the massif that forms the divide between the Saas and the Matter valleys. The former takes the trekker to Saas-Fee, 'the most beautiful village in the Alps' according to Sir Alfred Wills, one of those intrepid Britons who first dared to venture into the unexplored and mysterious terrain of the Alps. A High Court judge, Wills was also one of the original members of the world's first mountaineering association, the Alpine Club, in 1857. On the other side of the Mischabel, the Mattertal leads to Zermatt, the famous ski resort, which is surrounded by the most spectacular range of 13,000-foot peaks in Europe, including Monte Rosa, Lyskamm (nicknamed the *Menschenfresser* or the 'man-eater') and Breithorn. The indisputable king, however, is the Matterhorn – at 14,690 feet, its black pyramidal silhouette casts a spell over the entire region.

During the nineteenth century these mountains – 'the cathedrals of the earth, with their gates of rock, pavements of cloud, choirs of stream and stone, altars of snow, and vaults of purple traversed by the continual stars', as the art critic and philanthropist John Ruskin described them in 1856 – were the Holy Grail for British climbers. Leslie Stephen, a prominent climber and father of Virginia Woolf, coined the expression 'playground of Europe' to illustrate the allure that the enigmatic glaciers, the yawning crevasses and the awe-inspiring snowy peaks exerted on the increasingly affluent British middle classes. All this happened during the Victorian period, when secluded, impoverished mountain hamlets such as Grindelwald and Zermatt became favourite destinations for wealthy tourists.

In the case of Zermatt, the history books usually mention two men as the driving force behind its prosperity. One is Alexander Seiler, an ambitious Swiss soap-maker with the vision to recognise the importance of comfortable accommodation in attracting British travellers. In 1854, Seiler bought the Hotel Mont Cervin and, after renaming it Hotel Monte Rosa, transformed it into one of the most luxurious establishments in the Alps, a status shared with The Bear Hotel in Grindelwald and the Hotel de Londres et d'Angleterre in Chamonix. In the following years, Seiler's new hotels established the foundations that transformed Zermatt into a thriving tourism location.

Zermatt is also largely indebted for its prominence to the London-born climber Edward Whymper. After eight failed attempts to climb the Matterhorn – 'there seemed to be a cordon drawn around it, up to which one might go, but no further' – on 14 July 1865, Whymper finally became the first person to stand on the summit. His achievement is usually considered to mark the end of the Golden Age of Alpinism, a period that stretched from 1854 to 1865 during which thirty-six summits above 12,000 feet were climbed for the first time, thirty-one of them by British parties. Whymper's feat, however, was marred by the death of four of his companions during the descent: a French guide, Michel Croz, and three Englishmen, Lord Francis Douglas, the Reverend Charles Hudson and Douglas Robert Hadow, a student from Cambridge with little climbing experience. During the descent, Hadow slipped and pulled the other three over the edge of a 4,000-foot precipice. In the aftermath of the accident many questions were raised regarding the circumstances, and in particular the strength of the rope that had snapped between the survivors and those who fell. It was even suggested that it had been deliberately cut, a claim that was subsequently proven to be untrue.

The Matterhorn Disaster, and the ensuing public interest in the motivations of climbers, put Zermatt and mountain climbing on the front page of every newspaper in the United Kingdom. Charles Dickens was one of the most prominent public figures to show incomprehension of the motives of climbers. The celebrated author expressed his disdain for the scientific arguments commonly used at that time to justify mountain climbing by noting that "the scaling of such heights contributes as much to the advancement of science as would a club of young gentlemen who should undertake to bestride all the weathercocks of all the cathedral spires of the United Kingdom". In any case, the controversy was a tremendous boost for Zermatt, proof of the observation that all publicity is good publicity.

★

The Alps are no longer the centre of the climbing universe. By the beginning of the twentieth century every peak in the range had been climbed. Only a few north faces remained unchallenged, the most notorious being that of the Eiger which was not successfully climbed until 1938. As a result, elite climbers started to turn their attention to mountain ranges elsewhere – the Caucasus, the Andes, and following the steps of the British expeditions to Mount Everest in the 1920s, the Himalayas and Karakoram.

Nonetheless, the popularisation of skiing and other winter sports in the inter-war period helped to maintain a steady flow of visitors to the Alpine resorts. This tendency intensified after World War II, and today Zermatt is a magnet for mass tourism from all over the world. During the summer season, when the slopes are depleted of snow, skiers and snowboarders are replaced by hordes of sightseers. After trekking in the mountains for a couple of weeks with hardly anyone in sight, the overcrowded streets of Zermatt always come as a shock – they are certainly not the ideal surrounding for those who, like me, relish the quietness and solitude of mountains. Yet, the view of the Matterhorn, majestic over the town, makes a visit to Zermatt an unforgettable experience.

The Matterhorn is probably the most recognisable mountain in the world. In fact, its name and image are used by a myriad of different commercial companies, from Swiss chocolate makers and Italian fashionable shoe designers to London-based literary agents and American equity fund firms. Even Disneyland has an attraction called *The Matterhorn Bobsleds* which faithfully replicates, although on a lesser scale, the shape of the mountain – the surrounding palm-trees being the only discord. Alas, nothing is perfect, not even in Disneyland.

As an international icon, much has been said and written about the Matterhorn over time. However, no one has captured its spirit and uniqueness better than Gaston Rébuffat, a French climber who in 1950 was part of the first team to climb a peak exceeding 26,000 feet – Annapurna, in the Himalayas. Maurice Herzog, the expedition leader once commented humorously that Rébuffat 'had a scandalous origin for a mountaineer, and even worse for a guide. He was born at the seaside! It would take the Company of Guides many years to live this down.' Regardless of his birthplace, Rébuffat was not only an outstanding mountaineer but also an extremely talented writer of more than twenty books. Written in a lyrical style that captures the imagination, *Men and the Matterhorn* is still, almost fifty years after its publication, a masterpiece of mountaineering and Alpine literature. One of the most poignant passages of the book describes how the mountain affected him:

Up to the age of twelve I had never been outside my native Provence; and yet, without being aware of it, I knew the Matterhorn. I did not know it by name, but I knew it. When, by chance, someone in my family uttered the word 'peak', and my small child's imagination created the corresponding picture, I saw a pyramid, beautiful as an arrow of stone, pointing towards the sky. Later in life, I have been up countless valleys to discover mountains of all shapes and heights, but have never come across any like the Matterhorn. I have also questioned climbers of all countries who have visited even more of the world's mountains than I have. They have never seen a mountain to compare with the Matterhorn either. Moreover, on reflection, no one arriving at Zermatt or coming up from Châtillon to Breuil has ever exclaimed on seeing the Matterhorn for the first time, 'it looks like such and such a mountain'. Conversely, on approaching other peaks, how many times have we said, spontaneously and with a peculiar joy, 'Seen from here it looks like the Matterhorn.' No, the Matterhorn can resemble no other peak – it is the model; similarly, no other peak really resembles the Matterhorn; the mould has been broken, there are not even any copies. The Matterhorn is unique.

My wife, Marian, and I saw the Matterhorn for the first time after crossing the Col de Riedmatten during the eighth stage of the Haute Route, one of the most beautiful and demanding mountain treks in Europe. The Matterhorn was still more than fifteen miles away as the crow flies, yet its magnificent, gleaming triangular shape overshadowed all other mountains in sight around us. We stayed for only a few moments in that exposed, wind-battered pass, but during that time I was unable to take my eyes away from it.

The Haute Route, so named because it traverses mountain trails mostly above 6,000 feet, links Chamonix, on the French side of the Mont Blanc massif, and Zermatt, in the Swiss Valais. During ten days in the summer of 2012 we covered its 130 miles, weaving from one valley to the next, moving on a west-to-east course. It was an exhilarating journey; a daily succession of wonders during which we crossed fourteen mountain passes, six of them above 10,000 feet. In addition to the grandeur of the sky-scraping peaks that accompanied us along the entire route, every stage of the trek revealed new delights, from secluded emerald lakes, to the gravity-defying acrobatics of a herd of chamois, or the awe-inspiring desolation of the glaciers.

However, the trip was also a reminder that mountains have a dark and more sinister side. We experienced one such moment when the warm breeze of a cloudless afternoon turned into a freezing gale in a matter of minutes. The temperature dropped sharply, and, defying all forecasts of good weather, an ugly mass of black thunderheads raced towards us like a roaring monster. Soon the brightness of the day had turned to twilight, and the violent deluge that followed, dense and cold as a metal curtain, obliterated our view of the path in front of us. To speed up our pace, which would have increased the danger of slipping and falling over the precipice on our left, was out of the question. As we were above the tree line, being hit by lightning was also a very real possibility. There was nothing we could do but to stay calm and look for shelter. Thus, huddled together under our ponchos behind some rocks, we waited for the storm to pass. The prospect that the downpour could continue for hours was distressing as Marian, soaked from head to toe, was already shivering uncontrollably, and the nearest hut was more than a four-hour trek away.

Luckily, forty-five minutes later, and as suddenly as it had arrived, the tempest abated, with a return of the sunny skies that had accompanied us earlier. We resumed our journey and soon we were completely dry, as if the storm had only been a bad dream. That night, in the refuge, and sitting at a table next to ours, a couple of climbers in their early twenties were discussing the best route to ascend Mont Collon. Overhearing their conversation, I couldn't help but think of what could have happened if we had been on a sharp, snowy ridge when the storm hit, instead of the relative safety of a well-trodden mountain path.

On arriving in Zermatt, we decided to stay for a few days to relax and treat ourselves. We had no plans other than to sleep late, enjoy a good book on a sunny terrace and, finally freed of our heavy rucksacks, to walk around at leisure. On one of those lazy afternoons we visited the Mountaineers' Cemetery.

The night before we had been chatting with the couple who owned the hotel we were staying at – Leni and Thomas Müller-Julen – and at some point the conversation gravitated towards an accident that had taken place on Mont Maudit (in English, 'cursed mountain') several days earlier, in which nine climbers had perished in an avalanche. All were experienced alpinists, including Roger Payne, one of the most respected climbers in Europe, who was guiding some of the unfortunate climbers. When they set off early from the mountain hut, weather conditions were optimal. Apparently no technical mistakes had been made but a falling serac (a column of glacial ice), predictable in its unpredictability, had broken free and caused the accident.

I recall discussing with Leni and Thomas how difficult it was for me to grasp why people were so willing to risk their lives just to stand for a few minutes on the top of a mountain. My comment, however, didn't seem to make any sense to them, and they stared at me as if I were questioning why the sun rises every morning or why swallows fly. Born and bred in Zermatt, climbing mountains or exploring glaciers was for Leni and Thomas as natural as walking or breathing. In fact, Leni's father had been a famous guide in

21

the fifties and she, in her youth, had also climbed the Matterhorn several times. "You should visit the Mountaineers' Cemetery," she suggested, before adding, "Perhaps you will find answers for some of your questions there."

The Mountaineers' Cemetery is the resting place for the many of the climbers who, since the early nineteenth century, have perished while climbing in the Zermatt vicinity. It is also a powerful reminder of the perils of the mountain… of any mountain in the world. Situated behind the Catholic church of St Peter's, the graveyard is only a few yards away from the Monte Rosa Hotel and the hustle and bustle of Bahnhofstrasse, Zermatt's main street. Yet, it is a surprisingly quiet place. At least this is how Marian and I remember it – perhaps we simply didn't pay attention to the hubbub outside because we were so absorbed in reading the headstones. Some were extremely moving and I particularly recall the shivers down my spine when we came across the inscription of Herbert Braum and Anni Marschner, a German couple who fell to their deaths from the Hörnli ridge during their honeymoon in July 1924.

On the gravestone of Jonathan Conville, who died in 1979 on the north face of the Matterhorn, we read verses by Wilfrid Noyce, a member of the 1953 British expedition that made the first ascent of Mount Everest, who was himself killed some years later, on Mount Garmo, in what today is Tajikistan, Central Asia:

> Let me go climb these virgin snows,
>
> Leave the dark stain of man behind,
>
> Let me adventure and heaven knows,
>
> Grateful shall be my quiet mind.

I also vividly recall the grave of Donald Williams, a New Yorker who died on the Matterhorn in 1975. His epitaph was very short

– just four words. Yet, it made a strong declaration of principles, as if he was continuously responding to by-passers who, like us, were left wondering about the futility of his death. In a defiant manner, it read: "I chose to climb." He was 17 years old.

Then, another memorial attracted our attention. At first sight it was no different to many others in the cemetery, bearing a simple rectangular bronze plaque with two blazons on it. One of them depicted a crowned, rampant lion. The inscription read:

> *To the memory of William Bell, Ian McKean, and James Ogilvie, friends from Oxford killed together on the Matterhorn July 25th, 1948.*

Below, in Latin, was added *Non enim accessistis ad tractabilem montem* – 'For you are not come to a mountain that might be touched.'

Looking at their dates of birth, I made a rapid calculation of their ages: at 24, William was the oldest of the trio, while Ian was 22 and James 23. "They were almost kids," said Marian. I read the inscription twice – 'friends from Oxford killed together in 1948' – as if I were unable to comprehend the meaning or the magnitude of what I had before my eyes. There was something profoundly heart-rending for me in those words, an intense sense of closeness that even today is difficult to explain. Whatever it was, I was deeply moved by it.

We stood in silence in front of the inscription for a few seconds. Over the previous months, I had lived and breathed the Haute Route. I had studied countless times the various stages of the trek, the accommodation options, the travelling plan and so on. Although I didn't know anything about the three young men in their final resting place in front of me, it was not difficult to envisage them more than sixty years earlier, talking passionately about the grandeur of the mountains, analysing together the technical difficulties that awaited them on their way to the Matterhorn summit, preparing their climbing equipment or simply sitting in a pub, discussing animatedly the logistics of the trip to Switzerland. That was easy to imagine. The difficult part, however, was reconciling that vision of them, filled with youthful enthusiasm, with what the cold bronze plaque so mercilessly proclaimed – that none of them had returned from the mountain alive that day.

At that moment, it also occurred to me that, despite their youth, it was possible that they had fought for their King and country during World War II, which had ended barely three years earlier. If that was the case, it meant that they had survived the immense collective catastrophe of the war only to die together when peace had been restored, with their lives stretched out before them. I recall saying to Marian that life sometimes could be infinitely cruel.

I don't know why, but at that moment I felt the urge to find out more about William, Ian and James – about their short lives, about their dreams and aspirations, but also their love of the mountains and the invisible bond that brought them together to the Matterhorn, and which had finally sealed their fate. In hindsight, I guess I was so moved by the death of these hitherto strangers because somehow I saw my own passion and craving for life reflected in theirs. The fact that they came from Oxford, where I live, definitely contributed to my motivation. However, these are just *a posteriori* attempts to rationalise the emotions that washed over me that afternoon in Zermatt's Mountaineers' Cemetery. The truth is that I am unable to describe *why* I was so deeply moved. There I was, surrounded by scores of headstones, each of them describing a personal tragedy, and yet one in particular, with three names I had never heard of before in my life, touched me in a way that is impossible to explain.

Three unknown names on a bronze plaque in a foreign cemetery – that is how this story starts.

2. *From Oxford to Mount Kenya*

I travel not to go anywhere, but to go.
Robert Louis Stevenson

A couple of days after returning to England, I met my friend Diego at Georgina's, a cosy café popular with students situated in the Covered Market, in the heart of Oxford. Diego is a lecturer in Economics at St Anthony's, one of Oxford University's postgraduate colleges and, like me, he had recently returned from abroad, in his case from Guatemala, where he had been carrying out some research for most of the summer. Normally we would have spent the afternoon catching up or discussing the latest events in the tiny Central American nation, a place I know quite well as I did part of my PhD research there, or simply putting the world to rights. Not that day; instead, a large part of the conversation revolved around the cemetery in Zermatt and the intense emotions that had overwhelmed me while reading the stories engraved on its tombstones. Diego listened to my account of the events with a mixture of interest and curiosity, and when I showed him a picture of the grave of William Bell, Ian McKean and James Ogilvie he agreed that there was indeed something truly appealing about it. It was then that the eureka moment happened. "They look like the arms of a college of the university," Diego said, pointing at the two blazons in the bronze plaque. He paused, and with a wide grin of satisfaction he added, "In fact, the more I look at them the more certain I am that the second one, the one with the lion on it, is Balliol's."

I mentally cursed myself for my blindness. For two days I had been looking at the picture of the tombstone and that possibility had not crossed my mind, not even for a second. To rub salt into the wound, Balliol College is one of my favourite places in Oxford. I even slip in there sometimes at lunchtime. Certainly I don't do it for the food, which is just the kind of average stuff that can be found in any student canteen, but because the place is a feast for the eyes. The imposing stone fireplaces at each side of the room; the wood-panelled walls covered with old portraits of former masters and notable alumni, most of them stern-looking as if they had never had an iota of fun in their lives; the magnificent organ in the gallery over the main door; and the stained-glass windows through which the sun's rays acquire a delicate, almost unreal texture – everything in Balliol's dining hall helps to create an entrancing atmosphere. Even if they served beach pebbles for lunch, the place would still be worth a visit, with a good book as a companion, to leave behind the stress of a busy morning.

It was almost nine in the evening when I said goodbye to Diego and the city was already flooded with the translucent, silky twilight. I walked the short distance that separates the Covered Market from Balliol's main entrance in Broad Street. Diego was right – there it was, above the lintel of the college gate, the blazon with the rampant lion.

On my way home the alleyways that surround All Souls College were completely empty and calm, as if everybody else in the world had suddenly vanished. Beyond Christ Church Meadow, the Isis flowed effortlessly, with the same Arcadian civility that infuses the whole town. I recall thinking how much I loved Oxford, a place devoted to culture and learning for more than a thousand years: a cradle that had nurtured some of the principles that shape Western culture as we know it today and where past and present embrace traditions and customs, rather than being in conflict with them.

At that moment the verses of Gerard Manley Hopkins – himself a former Balliol student and one of the most important poets of the Victorian period – came to my mind:

Towery city and branchy between towers; cuckoo-echoing, bell-swarmed; lark-charmed, rock-racked, river-rounded.

★

That night I had trouble falling asleep. Like a six-year-old child in a sugar-high trance after eating too many sweets, I was over-excited by the possible connection between Balliol College and the three young climbers. Since returning home I had been looking for information about them – I had tried searching the Internet for details of their lives or the accident, but alas nothing at all had come up. In fact, after quite a few unsuccessful hours in front of the computer, I had even started considering the gloomy possibility that the search might end even before it had properly begun. Hence the adrenaline rush that the clue leading me to Balliol had produced.

First thing the next morning, I called the college's Alumni Office to find out if they had any information about William Bell, Ian McKean and James Ogilvie. I was aware that mine was an unusual request, to say the least. Of course, I knew my motives were genuine, but I was not certain whether the person at the other end of the line would understand why I had felt so moved by the tombstone of some people killed in an accident more than sixty years earlier. The worst and not very unlikely scenario was that he or she would think I was a snooper, prying into someone else's disgrace, and refuse to give me any information on the basis I was not a relative.

With that daunting prospect in mind, I heard the telephone ring a few times. I was certainly nervous; so much that when a female voice responded, for a fraction of a second I thought about hanging up. Thankfully I didn't, as the person who answered the phone, Janet Hazelton, couldn't have been more helpful. After explaining how I had come across the tombstone of William, Ian and James, she initially told me that she couldn't help me because they had already passed away. For that reason, rather than contacting the Alumni Office, I should have directed my request to the college's archivist. I don't remember what I said at that point, but I think she sensed the profound tone of disappointment in my voice because she still kindly offered to take a look at the college's registry for me. I carefully spelt out the three names and, after a minute or so that seemed to last an eternity, she returned to the line to say, "Yes, here they are: James Ian Campbell McKean, born on October 3rd 1925, and James William Ogilvie, born on January 25th 1925. Both of them were students and came to read Classics at Balliol."

Unfortunately she did not find anything about William Bell.

Janet promised to send me a copy of the registry by email. I don't know how many times I said thank you before hanging up, but surely there were a few of them. Her message came later that morning. The entries for James and Ian did not contain more than four or five lines each, but reading them was as exciting as opening a treasure chest.

James Ogilvie turned out to be the son of Sir Frederick Wolff Ogilvie, the director-general of the BBC from 1938 to 1942 and later principal of Jesus College in Oxford. Apparently a very popular teacher, Sir Frederick was one of the first academics in Britain to explore the impact of tourism on the economy. James had attended Rugby School and, in 1944, after spending one year at Balliol, had joined the army aged nineteen. He served with the Royal Scots Greys as a private and was wounded in April 1945 in Germany. James returned to Oxford in September 1947. The accident on the Matterhorn happened during his first summer as a civilian after the end of the war.

The registry information about Ian McKean was also very interesting. He was born in Sanderstead, Surrey, but the whole family was moved to the seaside village of Rustington, Sussex, in 1939 when his father's office (Ian's father was an engineer) was evacuated from London to Hove. As a boy, he attended Tonbridge School and in 1944 he joined the army. Unlike James, Ian did not go into combat as he was assigned to the Intelligence Corps. In 1946, after he was demobilised with the rank of captain, he returned to Balliol to read Classics.

For the rest of the day I could barely stop smiling. Not only had I finally got some information about Ian and James, but my hunch about them having served in the army during World War II was right. If the information contained in the registry was accurate, James would have even participated in one of the most important episodes of the war – Operation Market-Garden. Planned by General Montgomery, its goal was to bring forward the end of the war in Europe by four or five months. With the German armies in the Western Front in constant retreat after D-Day, the Allied forces tried to perform a bold move across Holland that, after taking several strategically important bridges between Eindhoven and Arnhem, would allow them to penetrate into Germany by the Lower Rhine. James' unit, the Royal Scots Greys – one of the most legendary British cavalry regiments with a service record stretching back beyond the Napoleonic Wars and Waterloo – was actively involved in the fights that led to the liberation of Eindhoven and the capture of Nijmegen Island and the Wilhelmina Canal.

Operation Market-Garden was popularised by the superb movie, *A Bridge Too Far*, which I must have seen dozens of times when I was a child, on lazy Saturday afternoons when the TV was full of movies of pirates, cowboys and soldiers, and the good guys always prevailed. One of my favourite moments in the film is when Lieutenant Colonel Frost (played by Sir Anthony Hopkins), who was leading the British paratroopers in the assault on the Arnhem Bridge, asked one of his officers why, when in combat, he always carried an umbrella. The man's response was that he did it because he could never remember the password, and it would be quite obvious to anyone that the bloody fool carrying the umbrella could only be an Englishman.

Years later, I learned that this was not a fictional episode made up by a Hollywood script-writer but was actually inspired by real events. The umbrella-holder, Major Allison Digby Tatham-Warter, was Frost's second-in-command and despite being injured and captured by the Germans, he managed to escape and return to Allied lines. Others were not so lucky. Operation Market-Garden failed to achieve its objectives and James' Royal Scots Greys, alongside many other Allied units, sustained a dramatic number of casualties.

The second blazon, which I was now sure could lead me to William Bell, was still an uncracked nut – the Jacobean pilgrim shell on a Saint Andrew's cross did not match any of the other university colleges' arms. The search online had failed to produce any positive results either. I was down what looked like a blind alley and it seemed obvious that new sources of information would be required.

One avenue potentially worth exploring was whether, back in 1948, William, Ian and James had belonged to any climbing club or society. By its very nature, climbing is a gregarious activity in which you not only constantly rely on your partners' skills and strength, but also often trust your life to them. This, inevitably, creates strong bonds of friendship between fellow climbers. Take, for example, what Charles Edward Mathews, an original member of the Alpine Club and its president between 1878 and 1880, said of Melchior Anderegg, one of the most famous guides at the time, "To say that I owe him a debt impossible to pay is not to say much … He first taught me how to climb … For more than twenty years he has led me. Year after year I have met him with keener pleasure. Year after year I have parted from him with a deeper regret."

The sociable side of climbing is manifested in many other ways too. Like fishermen gloating about their catches, climbers love talking about the mountains that they have climbed, the route's they've tried, successes, failures, and future plans. Ask any of them what they enjoy most about their sport and you'll hear familiar answers: conversations with colleagues in camp before and after a climb, the atmosphere of camaraderie between members of an expedition, or simply having a beer in a pub with friends after a day in the hills.

Climbing clubs and societies, as well as fostering that camaraderie, provide an opportunity to learn from more experienced members. They are, therefore, an ideal way to improve your skills and learn new techniques. Since the Matterhorn is by no means a walk in the park – you don't wake up one morning in Zermatt saying to your friends, "Hey, this mountain looks nice, what if we go up there?" – and considering that James and Ian were students at the time of the accident, I thought that the Oxford University Mountaineering Club, or OUMC, one of the oldest university climbing clubs in the UK, was the perfect place to start my quest.

According to Andrew Ross, the unofficial historian of the OUMC, the club was created in March 1909 by Arnold Lunn, the son of Sir Henry Lunn, the founder of Sir Henry Lunn Travel and a pioneer in the organisation of the first all-inclusive tourist trips from Britain to the Swiss Alps. Having been raised in Grindelwald, at the foot of the Eiger, Lunn was a gifted climber with a strong passion for mountains that would inspire his whole life. "When I was a small boy," he wrote, "I had no ambition to be a soldier or an engine-driver. Life, to me, began and ended with mountains." In the early years of the OUMC, the activities of the club were mainly social, with slide shows and dinners as the main events. It was only after World War I that climbing trips began to be organised in the Lake

District and North Wales on a regular basis over the Christmas and Easter vacations, and in the Alps in the summer. During the weekends, the bridges and steep tunnel walls of the railway line at Horspath, about five miles south-east of Oxford, were a popular training venue for club members.

Nowadays, the OUMC website contains many interesting bits of information about the club's climbing activities, social life and the like. Alas, it does not have what I was looking for: former members' records, old journals and so on. To access them, I was told, it would be necessary to visit the Oxford Mountaineering Library, jointly maintained by the OUMC and the Bodleian Library. It was mid-August, only five days after I had returned from Zermatt, but unfortunately a library visit would have to wait for at least two weeks, as the next morning I was due to travel to Bolivia for professional reasons.

Situated at almost 13,000 feet above sea level, Bolivia's capital, La Paz, is a magical place. The sky, for example, is an extravagant blue colour, and hangs over your head as if you were surrounded by a solid but at the same time weightless dome. It is a thrilling town, full of kind and cheerful people, but also possessed by a tormented soul. In La Paz, ancient gods and pagan demons dance in front of the Virgin Mary during religious processions; shoeshine boys hide their faces behind black masks, and children as young as six or seven years old wait at midnight outside cinema doorways – not to beg for money but for remains of soda you didn't drink. A city of huge contrasts, above all it is a place that I adore – I lived there for three years in my late twenties and it is still like home to me.

Mountains are an essential feature of La Paz. The city is built inside a cauldron-shaped valley of steep walls dominated by the splendid triple-peaked Illimani, which towers up to 21,122 feet.

Like a mammoth version of the Lighthouse of Alexandria – one of the Seven Wonders of the Ancient World, whose light could be seen as far as 100 miles away – the perpetual snows of the Illimani are perfectly visible from every single corner of La Paz. Outside the city, the rough, treeless plateau known as Altiplano offers the visitor a moon-like landscape, the endless horizon only broken by one of the most splendid mountain ranges in the world, the Cordillera Real, which is part of the Andes. The combination of the inhospitable flatness of the Altiplano and the ochre-and-white flamboyance of the Cordillera creates a bamboozling vision, like a mirage created by some playful, naughty mind.

The journey to Bolivia was a long one – almost twenty-four hours from London, including a lengthy transit in Miami. On the bright side, it was a good opportunity to get some quality reading time. The book I took with me was *No Picnic on Mount Kenya* by Felice Benuzzi, the story of one of the most incredible mountaineering feats ever undertaken. In 1939, at the outbreak of World War II, Felice was a young Italian civil servant working for the colonial administration in Abyssinia (the current Ethiopia), which had been invaded by Mussolini's troops four years earlier. When the Italians were defeated by the British forces advancing north from Kenya at the end of 1941, Felice, together with other civilians, was sent to a prison camp. His destination was Nanyuki, not far from the base of Mount Kenya (17,057 feet). In the book, Felice describes how, after many months of a dull life and absolute boredom at the camp, he and two fellow Italians escaped their imprisonment to climb what even today is considered a very dangerous peak. Leaving a note telling the British Compound Officer '...not to worry, we'll be right back as soon as we climb the mountain,' the trio sneaked out of their prison with bags full of makeshift gear fabricated from whatever scraps they could find in the camp, and some meagre rations that they had managed to save. They did it – they climbed a mountain that had previously repelled some of the world's best-equipped and most expert mountaineers. Amazingly, they not only climbed it so poorly equipped but also without using any kind of map. In fact, the only source of information they possessed, other than their own observations from the camp, was a drawing of Mount Kenya on the label of a tin of preserved meat that was distributed to the prisoners. Faithful to their promise, half-starved but jubilant, they returned to the prison after their feat.

The choice of *No Picnic on Mount Kenya* was not accidental. Most of the mountaineering books that can be found on the shelves of any book store are written by famous, professional climbers, whose entire lives are built around and dedicated to mountains. I read Benuzzi's book because I was trying to figure out why ordinary people, anonymous amateurs like William, Ian and James, feel so bound to climb mountains, accepting all the risks that come with that decision. In a way, I was also trying to understand why I never felt that longing.

Some answers to my questions were provided not by Benuzzi, but by his wife, Stefania, who forty years later, during an interview, said of her husband's exploits:

> *The war, the prisoners' camp, The Mountain: these were the three decisive elements in his life. The urge to be an independent individual and the love of freedom prompted him to take the risks of his adventure. He returned to the camp feeling at peace with himself and with his life, and writing the book filled days behind the barbed wire, until the end of the war. Ever since, The Mountain has accompanied us throughout our lives. Wherever we went, Mount Kenya was there, too.*

Felice and his companions did not climb Mount Kenya to gain fame or money. Nor did they do it in order to break any record or for more intangible reasons such as glory, honour or national pride. Their climb was the triumph of the human spirit, no more and no less – a way to prove to themselves that even in the most adverse circumstances, even inside a physical and mental prison, they were still capable of finding the inner strength necessary to prevail.

I finished *No Picnic on Mount Kenya* the day I left La Paz. That evening, at the airport, I contemplated in ecstasy how Illimani was burning red in the departing winter sun. At that moment I got a glimpse of the role that mountains could have also played in William, Ian and James' young lives when the words of John Tyndall, one of the key figures of the Golden Age of Alpinism, and the author of *The Glaciers of the Alps*, came into my mind:

> *Mountains have been to me well-springs of life and joy. They have given me royal pictures and memories which can never fade. They have made me feel in all my fibres the blessedness of perfect manhood, causing mind and soul and body to work together with a harmony and strength unqualified by infirmity or ennui...*

It is difficult for me to explain why, but I am sure that the three young men from Oxford would have treasured these words.

3. The library

The library card is a passport to wonders and miracles.
Libba Bray

The weather was glorious when I returned from Bolivia, which was a lovely surprise, considering the unremitting rain we had endured for most of the spring and summer. The following day I cycled to the Bodleian Library to get my membership card so I could get access to the OUMC library. The sky was cloudless and I was in high spirits – few things are as pleasant as riding through the streets of Oxford on a warm, sunny afternoon. If only there were fewer buses and cars in the city centre and, above anything else, fewer suicide-prone, absent-minded tourists all set to jump in front of your bike.

Located on the ground floor of the Clarendon Building, and not far from Balliol College, the Bodleian's Admissions Office has high roofs, walls painted in neutral colours and floor-to-ceiling windows that flood the room with natural light. Remarkably it was very quiet when I arrived, without any trace of the shipshape rowdiness that usually reigns in this type of office. The noise coming from the street was almost inaudible and the staff seemed to be very relaxed, almost under a kind of Zen, Oxford-style spell. I could not help but wonder whether the atmosphere would be so harmonious once the Michaelmas Term began a few weeks later, bringing with it the customary crowds of hyper-excited students.

Getting my membership card took no more than five minutes, at the end of which I was asked to recite aloud what sounded like a medieval oath – one of those small, ubiquitous details in Oxford that best reflect the city's love of tradition:

I hereby undertake not to remove from the Library, nor to mark, deface, or injure in any way, any volume, document or other object belonging to it or in its custody; not to bring into the Library, or kindle therein, any fire or flame, and not to smoke in the Library; and I promise to obey all rules of the Library.

With the pass in my pocket, I headed towards the OUMC library, on Parks Road, happy as an eight-year-old boy attending a game at his favourite football club for the first time. Like Odysseus in Cavafy's poem '*Ithaca*', I had the vague feeling that I was embarking on a trip towards an unknown destination. All I hoped was that the road ahead of me 'would be a long one, full of adventure, full of discovery'.

Dorothea Benton Frank, the American author, once said that librarians are like doctors, travel agents and professors all rolled into one. To me there is no better way to describe Sue Bird, a subject librarian at the Radcliffe Science Library, where the OUMC library is located. With her round spectacles and greying hair, like a skilled doctor she listened carefully as I told her why I was interested in William Bell, Ian McKean and James Ogilvie. Like a knowledgeable travel agent, she guided me through the countless bookshelves in the library, until we reached the safety of the mountaineering section. Finally, like a judicious professor, she recommended the best books for my research, with the clinical precision of someone who knew the whole catalogue by heart.

I stayed in the mountaineering section for about fifteen minutes or so, leafing through books here and there. Unfortunately, I could not stay much longer as my lunch break was quickly coming to an end. By the time I went back to my office, an email from Sue was already blinking in my computer's in-box. It said:

Dear Dr Cabello,

I continued to investigate your query after you left.

One thing we didn't consult was the various journals c̦ ......
time.

The accident is mentioned in the Alpine Journal vol. LVI,
no.277 (Nov. 1948) p. 405, "Three Oxford undergraduates,
who had set out guideless one Sunday in July, reached about
half-way on the Hörnli ridge when one of them is believed
to have slipped and dragged down the others."

I believe I'm correct in saying that the other crest depicted on
the plaque is that of Merton College.

With best wishes for your research,

Yours, Sue Bird

Sue's message was a bombshell. To begin with, she believed to have positively identified the other blazon as Merton's. If she was right, it could be a huge leap forward to establish who William Bell was. More importantly, her email gave me the first hint of what had allegedly happened on the Matterhorn in 1948. Short as it was, the Alpine Journal note contained two valuable pieces of information – it not only stated that the ascent had been attempted without the support of a professional guide, but it also suggested that the accident on the Hörnli ridge had happened after one of the three climbers had slipped, dragging the others with him.

The Hörnli ridge is one of the four arêtes that form the almost perfect pyramidal shape of the Matterhorn. This ridge is also considered to be the easiest way to the summit, which makes it a very popular option among climbers. Was there any relation between the choice of the route and the fact that William, Ian and James had decided to attempt the climb without a professional guide? If they were seasoned climbers, then it would make sense that they had tried to reach the summit on their own. The other possibility, though, was that they had recklessly underestimated the difficulty of the ascent as a result of their lack of experience. It was my wife who had suggested this latter option, 'Perhaps they bit off more than they could chew.' Although that was plausible, something that was necessary to bear in mind, somehow I resisted believing it.

The vagueness of the language used in the note to describe the accident – 'one of them is believed to have slipped' – also caught my attention. In mountaineering circles, the slip theory is usually the default answer provided when witnesses are not available and therefore it is impossible to establish how an accident has taken place. Was the ambiguity in the note an indication that nobody had seen what had actually happened? Today there are usually so many climbers on the Matterhorn that bottlenecks form in some sections, particularly those with fixed ropes put in place by the guides. But in 1948 there were no fixed ropes, and if the weather was not good then it is likely that there were few other people on the mountain – in which case the lack of witnesses would definitely make sense. I made a note to remind myself to check the weather report for that day.

The note also seemed to suggest that they were roped together when they fell to their deaths. While a three-man rope is not an entirely unusual configuration, it is sometimes riskier than the more typical two-man line. Communication among three climbers, for example, becomes more difficult than between two, which in turn increases the likelihood of making mistakes. Also, rate of progress is significantly slowed. Speed is critical on the Matterhorn – the less time you spend on its steep, narrow slopes, the less exposed you are to the unpredictable, fast-changing weather conditions on the mountain, especially on warm summer days when thunderstorms often build up in the afternoon. Speed is a critical factor for another reason – climbing and descending the

Hörnli ridge usually takes at least ten or twelve hours. Longer days produce more tired climbers, and the chance of making mistakes rises exponentially.

Later that day I called Merton and they confirmed that William Bell had indeed been a student there. A copy of the college registry arrived by email early that evening. The email also explained why it had been so difficult to identify Merton's blazon. Apparently, the coat of arms that appeared on the tombstone in Zermatt was not the 'official' one but rather a combination of Merton's and the coat of arms of the Bishop of Rochester, who founded the college in 1264.

William's entry made for a fascinating read. The son of a doctor, he was born in Shardlow, Derbyshire, in July 1924. Like Ian and James, he had served in the British armed forces during World War II, in his case as part of the Royal Naval Volunteer Reserve. A year older than his two friends, he first came to Oxford in 1942 to read Physics. By the time he returned after the war, in 1946, he had changed his mind and decided to read English instead. The real surprise was to learn that William was a poet. In fact, two books compiling his best works, *Elegies* and *Mountains Beneath the Horizon*, had been published in 1946 and 1950 respectively. Reading the registry, it was evident that he had been an active member of Oxford literary circles, as he had also edited two other books: *Poetry from Oxford in the Wartime* in 1945 and *More Poetry from Oxford* in 1947.

'A poet,' I recall thinking with satisfaction. In my eyes a poet had, necessarily, to be someone cultivated, with varied cultural interests and probably with a rich personality too: all of them very appealing qualities for William to possess. More importantly, though, thanks to Merton's registry, I now had information about all three boys from Oxford. For the first time I had a small glimpse of the real people behind the heretofore unknown names on the tombstone.

Little did I know that in the days to come this would be multiplied a hundredfold.

★

The OUMC library was completely empty when I returned the following Saturday. The truth is that I have never seen anybody else there during any of my frequent visits. A windowless basement, badly illuminated by fluorescent bars, it contains no computers or anything that may reveal that we are in the twenty-first century. On one side of the room, some old microfilm readers are gathering dust, while on the other side there are five rows of shelves packed with books. Also, the floor is crammed with boxes containing old documents and maps awaiting those inscrutable processes that librarians perform in order to render them accessible to readers. The library looks like one of those recurrent grey subterranean vaults in John le Carré's spy novels: definitely the kind of place where you can visualise George Smiley up to his neck in dusty folders, looking for a clue that may lead to the identification of a Soviet mole. Despite its decaying atmosphere, or perhaps because of it, I loved the Mountaineering Library from the very moment I set foot there.

The climbing journals are located at the end of the room, on a shelf against the wall. The majority of them come from abroad – from Switzerland, Italy, or France but also from the United States, Canada and New Zealand. The earlier editions, those published during the nineteenth and early twentieth century, are luxuriously bound in leather with gold leaf letters. By contrast, those from the 1950s onwards are cheaper paper editions, so tightly packed that many of them are completely stuck to each other. Like a collection of fossils, the journals are relics of a long-gone era, before the Internet, when mountain lovers had to wait patiently for the postman to deliver the new editions of their beloved publications. Standing there, my feelings oscillated between glee about having access to this colossal amount of information and the sad realisation that nobody had probably touched them in years.

The first thing on my to-do list that morning was to look for the edition of the Alpine Journal that Sue had mentioned in her email. Unfortunately it did not contain any more information than the bits that she had already sent me. After that I aimlessly wandered around, dipping into other journals and papers, always looking in their indexes for references to the Matterhorn or the 1948 accident. I found nothing else, not even a small note. As a consolation, I took great pleasure in looking at their pictures, as well as devoting a few moments to reading the old adverts for mountaineering gear or clothes. Without any doubt, my favourite one appeared on the inside front cover of the November 1964 edition of the Alpine Journal, depicting two mountaineers happily enjoying a feast on the top of a mountain. The text in the advert claims, 'Horlicks concentrated meals are made for people in a hurry, for every situation where space and weight are at a premium. The man-sized meals are so simple to prepare – just add water, simmer and eat. Horlicks meals are really sustaining, light and compact, convenient for every outdoor activity.' It concludes with the optimistic assertion, perhaps not quite worthy of Don Draper: 'It's made by Horlicks – it must be good!'

In addition to spending a wonderful couple of hours reading about mountaineering and climbing, something much more important happened that day. Twice I had checked the section containing the OUMC journals in the hope that the 1948 edition would have some information about the accident. But, alas, it appeared that the journal had not been published in 1948 or 1949. In fact, from 1947 it jumped straight to 1950. This felt like a bucket of icy water was slowly being poured over my head, as two years was surely too much of a time lapse to find any further reference to what had happened in Zermatt in July 1948. For that reason, I didn't even bother to open the 1950 edition. It was only twenty minutes before leaving that I returned to the OUMC section and finally started leafing through it. The foreword confirmed that indeed there were no 1948 and 1949 editions: "It is two years since the OUMC Journal was last published. We hope that this number will not provoke a fervent prayer for an even longer interval before the appearance of the next." According to the table of contents, the 1950 edition had nothing but the usual stuff – a few articles describing mountaineering expeditions to the Alps and Pyrenees, new climbing routes in Scotland, and so on. It was the last section, though, that caught my eye, as it was called '*In Memoriam*'. I opened it up, and could barely believe what I was seeing – the obituaries of William, Ian and James were there, right in front of my eyes!

Finding them was so unexpected that at that moment I felt like my legs were shaking with emotion and that they would not be able to hold me up for much longer. So, before doing anything else, I had to sit down and take a couple of deep breaths. Reading the obituaries was extremely touching. Of William it said, 'He was a poet in his whole outlook, as well as in expression' who, before his death, 'had published a good deal of verse in various journals'. To help the reader better understand who he was, it added that 'it was a standard joke that no meet was official unless William was on it. And the joke had a strong tinge of truth in it, in that no meet seemed complete without him. Everyone in the club knew him and all liked him. When he was there life was never dull.' At the end of William's obituary, signed by an unidentified 'R. M. V.', it said that William 'climbed for the pleasure that it gave to him and to others', and it concluded by saying that William was a 'steady and cautious climber'.

Ian was depicted as a person of 'great abilities, wide interests and immense energy'; someone 'utterly loyal and dependable'; a person whose 'hatred of inaction and ineffectiveness led him during his army service to take the road from touchline academic liberalism to the Labour Party, and from hill walking to climbing proper'. In fact, according to the document, Ian was the chairman of the Labour Club at the university. He was also intellectually brilliant. 'After three terms he obtained his First in Classical Honour Moderations. By the end of his first year's work for Greats it was clear that he was set to pull off a double First.' About his love for mountains, the author of the obituary said, 'no term for him was tolerable without its hours of climbing plans and no vacation complete without its climbing meet', concluding that 'unlike the majority of our generation of climbers, he approached the Alps thoroughly familiar with the classical books of mountaineering and thoroughly saturated with what, if that phrase had not been cheapened in torrents of empty and pretentious verbiage, we might have called the spirit of the hills'.

James was painted as a very down-to-earth person, someone for whom an 'impenetrable modesty was not a pose but an essential part of him'. The obituary described the respect and affection in which he was held at Rugby, as well as Oxford : 'all who came in contact with him knew at once he was a person of quite unusual worth'. Turning to James' relationship with the mountains, it said that 'in climbing, as in so much else, he had it in him to do great things: to magnificent physique and rare powers of endurance he added the spiritual qualities – courage, steadiness, sense of humour'. Interestingly, it also mentioned that in 1946 he had been an officer in the army in India, where he also began his mountaineering career, on the borders of Tibet.

The most moving part of the obituaries was the conclusion – 'Their death together is a loss not only to us who knew them but to the future.' Again I felt the same sense of togetherness, of camaraderie, that had made such a strong impact on me the first time I saw the tombstone in Zermatt.

'Friends from Oxford killed together,' I recalled.

The obituaries gave me something completely new about William, Ian and James. Until that moment, all I had got from the colleges' registries were objective, cold facts like their dates of birth, origins, the schools they had attended, details of their military records, and so on. Instead, the obituaries contained personal descriptions of them: intimate portraits written by people who had actually known them. People who loved them while they were alive and mourned them when they died.

I made a photocopy of the journal and left. The day was still warm and Parks Road had the tranquil atmosphere of a schoolyard on a summer afternoon. I walked slowly under the big maple trees in the street with the papers in my hand. I don't recall thinking about anything, but I felt a strange sense of sad elation. In front of Wadham College a Japanese girl smiled, making a 'V for Victory' sign with her fingers, while her boyfriend was taking countless pictures of her.

4. Heroes and villains

There are only three real sports: bullfighting, car racing and mountain climbing. All the others are mere games.
Ernest Hemingway

I returned to the library a couple of times over the following days and although I found new references to the accident none of them provided any additional or relevant information. Probably the most interesting was a yellowing newspaper clipping from *The Times* that said William, Ian and James had not hired a guide because they had run out of Swiss Francs. That possibility had not crossed my mind, though it added up once considered in the light of the grim reality of life in post-war Britain – regardless of the fact that the war had ended three years earlier, the national economy was still in tatters in 1948, and food and other basic products were severely rationed. Only that summer did bread come off ration, with sugar rationing ending in 1953 and meat in 1954. Ration books for petrol were in use until 1950. Queues, everywhere and for everything, were a common element in the lives of millions of Britons. In an atmosphere of extreme austerity, never was the proverb 'waste not, want not' better epitomised. Despite hosting the XIV Olympiad in the summer of 1948, London was still a bomb-cratered, scarred city. Above all, Britain was insolvent. As a result, severe restrictions on how much money travellers could take out of the country or change into foreign currency were strictly enforced. So it was entirely plausible that the lack of Swiss Francs played an important role in the boys' decision not to hire a guide.

Another interesting piece of information unearthed in those days was the identity of the person who had written William's obituary, and who had clearly known him quite well. R. M. V. turned out to be Richard 'Dick' Viney, the president of the OUMC in 1950. Like William, Dick died very young while ascending the east buttress of the Jägihorn, in the Bernese Oberland, in 1956. His partner, Tom Bourdillon, was also killed in the same accident. In 1953, Tom had been part of the British expedition that had climbed Mount Everest for the first time. Together with Charles Evans, Bourdillon spearheaded the first assault on the summit, coming within only 300 feet of reaching it. It was after this failed attempt that plan B, led by Edmund Hillary and Tenzing Norgay, was set in motion. Hillary and Tenzing reached the highest point of the Earth three days later, on 29 May 1953, instantly becoming household names; heroes of the twentieth century. In contrast, few people outside climbing circles have ever heard of Tom Bourdillon, let alone Dick Viney.

I read the obituaries a few more times during my visits to the library, and it was evident that William was a captivating, charismatic individual, equally liked and admired by his peers. Modesty also appeared to be one of his main virtues – 'to hear him talk one would have thought that he had been pulled up every rock climb he had ever done'. William's love for poetry and literature was also manifest in the words that Dick Viney dedicated to him. In the obituary, William was depicted as a dreamer: as someone enthralled by heights but for whom climbing standards, achievements and records, apparently, meant nothing. Judging by the amount of time he spent in the wilderness ('as much as three months in the year'), mountains were a kind of Promised Land to him, a place where he found happiness, comfort and inspiration.

The obituary of Ian, written by an unknown A.G.N.F., also presented him as a dreamer. However, unlike William, for whom peaks and hills seemed to be an ever-present state of mind, Ian's ambitions were more worldly – he aspired to make of Britain a better place to live in: something that he seemed to pursue with total dedication and enthusiasm. Undoubtedly, Ian was a son of his own time. For the majority of Britons the end of World War II represented a chance to transform the rigid social structures that had governed the country for so long – a chance for everybody to enjoy the same opportunities in life, regardless of their origin or class. Held less than two months after VE Day, the elections in July 1945 resulted in the defeat of the Conservative government led by Winston Churchill and a landslide victory for the Labour Party. Profound reforms, deemed by many as unthinkable before the war, were quickly approved and implemented. The reform process left few stones unturned. The law to create a free and universal health system – the NHS – was passed in 1946. Also that year the National Insurance Act was approved, which sought to protect the population, on the basis of universality, from the perils of sickness, unemployment and old age. Whole areas of the productive fabric were nationalised with the aim of securing full employment for a population that had so heavily suffered the effects of the economic crisis in the years preceding the war. Fields like education and housing were also fundamentally transformed.

Ian's obituary laid a lot of emphasis on his deeply ingrained social values, suggesting a connection between them and his Congregationalist principles. True to his hands-on nature, it was evident that Ian not only believed in the necessity of all these transformations but also wanted to be part of them. Becoming the chairman of the Labour Party at the University of Oxford was his way of contributing to the winds of change that blew across Britain.

Finally, James was a decorated veteran: he had been first in the line of fire in Holland in 1944, and again in Germany in 1945, where he had been wounded. Reading between lines, James appeared to be a genuine young man who never evaded his responsibility, no matter how taxing it could be. In addition to his physical strength, James also seemed to have a special sensibility for the arts – not only was he a talented musician but he also possessed 'significant acting abilities'. His ready smile and sense of humour were an important part of his character too, as the obituary highlighted. In a nutshell, James was essentially someone fun to be around. Above all, he was a person 'whose friendship was as valuable as it was easy to gain'. A key part of James' life that also caught my attention was that, as an army officer, he had been a first-hand witness to one of the defining moments of the twentieth century – the independence of the Indian sub-continent.

★

The first time I saw their tombstone in Zermatt I got the feeling that there was something truly special about the three young men buried there. Now I felt vindicated by what their obituaries had revealed about them. The intellectual, the politician and the soldier – William, Ian and James appeared to be much more than some random climbers that I could use as a reference to explore why some people feel the lure of mountains. To a certain extent, they seemed to embody some of the virtues and values – generosity, intellectual capacity, abnegation and courage – which, to me, represent the best of the British character. This is what finally convinced me to write their story. What until that moment had just been a possibility, a distant idea I loved playing with, became a firm decision there and then. It was the Romantic poet William Wordsworth who once said that a writer must 'fill the paper with the breathings of his heart'. The more involved I got with William, Ian and James, the more I learnt about them, the more intense that urge was.

So mesmerising their short lives were to me that, by comparison, the specific circumstances of their deaths suddenly became much less important. At some point during those days at the library, I even stopped looking for new information about the accident. Whether one of them had slipped and dragged the others down, or an avalanche had swept all of them away, suddenly became irrelevant. Their deaths, no matter how tragic, were just one moment in their entire lives. It was in the rest of their existence where the focus had to be put if I wanted to better appreciate their relationship with mountains. In the same way that every ascent is always followed by a descent, and both become integral parts of the same experience, the climbing and non-climbing facets in the lives of William, Ian and James were inseparable sides of the same coin: one could not be understood without the other.

During the initial stages of my research, I found that this holistic approach to climbers' lives is quite rare. Thus, in most cases, the media coverage of mountaineering news is full of cliché and shallow analysis. The treatment received by Alison Hargreaves is a good example. In May 1995, the Derbyshire-born climber became the first woman to climb Everest unaided and without oxygen, something that until that day only Reinhold Messner, seen by many as the best climber ever, had achieved. "Quintessentially the finest piece of high-altitude mountaineering" or "Alison of Everest" were just some of the ways in which the adulating British press referred to her after her accomplishment. When, less than three months later, she was killed during a storm while descending K2, veneration became vilification with numerous commentators accusing her of callous selfishness as she left behind two children aged six and four years old. *The Daily Express*, for example, published an article on 19 August that questioned whether Alison was a responsible mother. The editorial column of *The Independent*, despite honouring her general achievements, led with the title 'Should mothers climb mountains?'

In a different way, mountaineering literature also contributes to promoting an over-simplistic depiction of climbing. A quick glance at the list of best-sellers in this field shows that most of them revolve, in one way or other, around dramatic accidents and death on mountains. To a certain extent this is inevitable as risk is an intrinsic part of climbing. However, it is also true that drama and sensationalism are always important selling points. Whatever the reason for the profusion of books centred on the most extreme side of mountaineering, these epic tales of resilience and courage against all the odds, but also of pain, suffering and fatalities, constitute a fertile ground for creating a mythological universe filled with heroes. Climbers tend to be presented as unique individuals capable of going far beyond places that ordinary people could only dream of; mavericks who coolly step into the zone between life and death and execute impossible feats in exceptional circumstances; free-spirited souls who refuse to abide by the dictates of society. As a consequence, very often climbing is surrounded by a sort of mystic aura, like a forbidden temple, concealed from the non-climbing world by an impenetrable veil, whose hallowed ground could only be trespassed on by a few chosen ones.

Climbers, of course, are not demigods but regular people who just happen to have a gift for getting on top of things. However, very few books dare to talk about the human side of climbing and mountaineering; about the real people behind the heroes; about their flaws or the consequences of their acts for other people's lives. When they do, (*Dark Shadows Falling* by Joe Simpson, and Maria Coffey's *Where the Mountain Casts its Shadow* are the most notable exceptions), the portraits presented are quite unflattering – climbers come across as self-centred, obsessed, narcissistic people who often put their own personal ambitions before anything or anybody else: adrenaline junkies whose life makes no sense without the danger that comes with absurd, good-for-nothing challenges.

Heroes or villains? As usual, reality is much more complex. After all, climbers are only human. Despite being an outsider, I have the feeling that climbing cannot be reduced to a matter of life or death, make or break, black or white, without any consideration for the rest of the colour palette. Maybe for some professional climbers, eager to attract the attention of sponsors by pursuing the next almost-impossible deed, this is how life is. But that is not the reality for the invisible majority of mountain lovers. Summer after summer I have seen the Alpine paths in the Swiss Valais, the Italian Dolomites or Provence packed with climbers of all ages and skills. During the weekends, whole families head towards some rocky wall or steep slope, eager to enjoy a day in the outdoors doing what they cherish the most. For them, summiting a mountain has nothing in common with the picture of climbing usually depicted by books and newspapers.

That's why, during the initial stages of my quest, I found so refreshing the efforts made by some climbing stars to demystify their activity. One of them, Steve House, writes in his book *Beyond the Mountain* that 'climbing has shown me a courageous, strong side of myself, a beautiful bravery. Other days I have seen a pitiful weakness. I have watched myself crawl, belly-flat across a mountain landscape of fear.' In the same vein, Simone Moro, an Italian climber who specialises in winter ascents in the Himalayas, made me laugh when he declared in an interview that 'in mountaineering there are the same proportion of idiots as anywhere else.' In a world where egos are often as big as the mountains that climbers aspire to conquer, the words of Iñaki Ochoa de Olza, whose record includes climbing twelve of the world's fourteen highest mountains without oxygen ('I am no hero; a hero is the doctor that cured my mother's cancer – I am just a professional tourist') are truly an exception.

That is also why the information contained in the obituaries about William, Ian and James was so appealing – they were not presented as fallen heroes but as naturally complex, multi-layered human beings who deeply loved mountains and just happened to die on one of them.

So, when I started thinking about the best approach to the story I wanted to write, one thing was clear in my mind: this was never going to be a book constructed around the accident on the Matterhorn. In fact, there are already too many tombstones in little cemeteries across the Alps telling that sort of story. I didn't want to write about bad luck, poor weather conditions on the mountain that day, nor better or worse climbing skills; speculating about the factors leading to the death of William, Ian and James was not only useless but, in my opinion, also showed a total lack of respect for them. Instead, in my view, the right thing to do was to focus on something that the three men from Oxford seemed to have in abundance: passion. Passion for poetry, for music, for their country, for their ideals and aspirations; passion for mountains; passion for life. Passion because passion is the common language that every person in love with heights shares and understands, whether he or she is an aficionado or a media darling.

The novelist Antonio Muñoz Molina says that a writer is not a person looking for stories, but someone who has received them in one way or other, and feels gratitude for the gift as well as the need to share it. This is how I felt when I decided to put on paper the story of William Bell, Ian McKean and James Ogilvie. Weird as it may sound, I always have had the impression that something was gently pushing me to write it, as if somehow the story had chosen me rather than the other way around. How else can I explain that among all the tombstones in the Mountaineers' Cemetery in Zermatt – all of them with their own dramatic account – my eyes turned to that of William, Ian and James? How else can I explain all the inexplicable things that happened to me in the following months?

Yes, this is definitely the best way to put it: as if the story had chosen me...

5. The legacy of Sandy Irvine

It is not in the stars to hold our destiny but in ourselves.
William Shakespeare

Great stories, those that remain forever as part of the collective memory of a society, usually contain good portions of mystery and tragedy. Take Jack the Ripper, for example. There have been other prolific serial killers before and after him but none of them have his magnetism. His status as a mega-star of crime (a position that he still holds today, judging by the number of books that are published about him every year) is mostly due to the fact that he was never captured – he simply vanished into thin air after killing his last victim, Mary Jean Kelly, in November 1888. It is the mystery surrounding his identity that keeps the legend alive. A good dose of tragedy is also indispensable to create a powerful story. Imagine if Romeo and Juliet's plans to escape to Mantua after Friar Laurence married them had succeeded and they had lived happily ever after. It wouldn't be the same, would it? Jean Valjean, Heathcliff, or Hamlet – the fact that they are all great characters has a lot to do with their tragic existence, and vice versa.

The story of George Mallory and Andrew 'Sandy' Irvine contains its fair share of mystery and tragedy as well. They disappeared in June 1924 on the north-east ridge of Mount Everest when they were spearheading the third British attempt in four years to conquer the highest mountain on Earth. For the members of the expedition, the dream of stepping up on top of the Everest represented much more than a mountaineering challenge – it was duty: a matter of national pride. The 'third pole', as it was known at the time, after the North Pole had been allegedly reached for the first time by Americans in 1909 and the South Pole by the Norwegians two years later, was seen by many as a British mountain. Therefore, the privilege to reach its summit before anybody else belonged to British climbers and to British climbers alone. For Sir Francis Younghusband, the president of the Royal Geographic Society, climbing Everest also represented a unique opportunity to lift the morale of a nation prostrated by the effects of the Great War and galvanise its population with the electric shock of doing what no one else had achieved before. "The accomplishment of such a feat will elevate the human spirit. It will give men a feeling that we really are getting the upper hand on the Earth, that we are acquiring a true mastery of our surroundings", he declared in 1920. According to Wade Davis, the author of *Into the Silence*, Britain, a desperate nation at the end of the war, embraced the assault on the summit of Everest as a 'gesture of imperial redemption'.

The preparations for the 1924 expedition, expected to be the definitive one, were executed with military precision. By early June, after several months of hard work, everything was ready for the final push. On the morning of 8 June, Mallory and Irvine left Camp VI, at 27,000 feet, on their way to the summit. They never returned. The last person to see them alive was Noel Odell, another member of the expedition who was at Camp V. He wrote in his diary:

> There was a sudden clearing of the atmosphere and the entire ridge and final peak of Everest were unveiled. My eyes became fixed on one tiny black spot silhouetted on a small snow-crest beneath a rock-step in the ridge; the black spot moved. Another black spot became apparent and moved up the snow to join the other on the crest. The first then approached the great rock-step and shortly emerged at the top, the second did likewise. Then the whole fascinating vision vanished, enveloped in cloud once more.

Today, almost a century later, the question of whether they reached the summit is still wrapped in mystery. If so, they would have beaten Edmund Hillary and Tenzing Norgay to the top of the world by nearly thirty years. History books should necessarily be modified, although most experts agree that first ascents should only be credited to climbers who get down safely as well as up. This was also the opinion of Mallory's son, John, who was only three years old in 1924. To him, the failure of his father to return home provided all the answers he needed. "To me, the only way you achieve a summit is to come back alive. The job is only half done if you don't get down again," he declared years later.

Whatever happened that day on the Everest, Mallory and Irvine were mourned as national heroes, and their memorial service at Saint Paul's Cathedral in October 1924 was attended by King George V, members of the Royal Family, the Prime Minister, and the entire British Cabinet.

In the eighties and nineties, several expeditions were organised in an attempt to locate and recover the bodies of Mallory and Irvine, as it was believed they could contain clues shedding light on what came to be known as the 'Mystery of Everest'. The most coveted item was the vest-pocket Kodak camera that they had with them – had they reached the summit they would have taken pictures, and given the good conditions in which the cameras would have been preserved on the mountain, it was likely that the films could still be developed. Finding the two bodies on the treacherous slopes of Everest proved to be not an easy task, though.

The most important clue about their whereabouts was an ice axe, found in 1933, with three score marks on the shaft, which the Irvine family later said were the same as he used to mark other items. And, of course, there was Odell's inconclusive report – he initially wrote in his diary that the two figures he saw that morning when the mist lifted were passing the second rock step, one of the formidable rock walls on the ridge. However, years later, Odell modified his testimony and said, "I could not be precisely certain at which of the two steps they were." Another lead came in 1979 when the Chinese climber Wang Hung-bao told a member of the Japanese Alpine Club that he had seen the body of a European on the north face of Everest during a climb in 1974. As foreigners were not given access to that side of the mountain after 1948, and no fatal accidents had been reported in the area other than that of 1924, the body could only belong to Mallory or Irvine. Unfortunately, three days after the conversation, Wang died in an avalanche and never had the opportunity to give a more precise report.

In 1999, seventy-five years after the fatal accident, Mallory's body was finally located, face down, head almost completely buried in scree, with a golf-ball-sized puncture wound on his forehead. All signs pointed to a fall as the cause of his death. The cameras were not found, but circumstantial evidence suggests that they could indeed have reached the summit. For example, his snow goggles were found in his pocket, which would indicate that he was not using them when he fell. In other words, the accident would have taken place at sunset, on their way to the camp, maybe after reaching the summit. According to Mallory's daughter, her father also took with him a picture of his wife, which he planned to leave on Mount Everest if he succeeded. Many documents were recovered from the well-preserved body of Mallory but there was no picture. This could indicate that he left the picture on top of Mount Everest.

Irvine's body has never been found.

This introduction is important because the story of William, Ian and James is intertwined with that of 'Sandy' Irvine. Like William a quarter of a century later, Irvine attended Merton College where, not surprisingly, he was an extremely popular student. Athletic and good-looking, he was a member of the Oxford rowing crew in 1922 and 1923 – the latter being the only occasion on which the Oxonians had beaten Cambridge since 1913. However, Sandy Irvine was much more than an outstanding athlete; his engineering skill was one of the most important factors taken into consideration when the Everest Committee selected him to be part of the expedition. During the trip he became responsible for the oxygen equipment, which was seen as the cornerstone of any successful attempt to reach the summit. After his death, his family created a trust with the aim of providing grants for Merton students who wanted to spend their holidays climbing or doing other mountaineering activities either in Britain or abroad.

The first time I heard about this fund was when Julian Reid, Merton's archivist, mentioned it after I called him to explore whether the college's library could contain information about William. Julian found my story fascinating and promised to provide as much help as possible. It was during that initial conversation that he suggested that perhaps the Irvine Fund had made a contribution to finance William's trip to the Alps in 1948. A couple of days later, I visited Merton to check that lead.

That Oxford is a charming place is indisputable. Whether it is beautiful or not is a different matter, though. Thus, the uninformed visitor will be surprised to find a town sober and modest in its external appearance. Forget the extravagance of the open-air museum that is the centre of Florence; tourists visiting Oxford will find no grand arched squares, sumptuous palaces or splendid civic buildings like those that can be enjoyed in Bruges, Rome or Lisbon. Do not go to Oxford expecting to rejoice in anything remotely similar to the colossal architecture of London, the classic elegance of Bath, or the chaotic, albeit captivating, exuberance of Edinburgh. No, Oxford is nothing like that. With the exception of a small area surrounding the Radcliffe Camera – the circular building with a lofty dome that is its most iconic image – the city centre is formed by an unappealing maze of cobbled streets and alleyways. Like an oyster that cherishes a delicate pearl under its rough ugly surface, the real beauty of Oxford can only be found inside the high, naked walls of its colleges.

Merton's library is a perfect example of this. Located in the south corner of Mob Quad, a four-sided group of edifices dating from 1373, it is the oldest continuously functioning library for university students in the world. Inside the building, the reading rooms are cosily illuminated, the red leather of the chairs is soft and pleasant to the touch and the wall-to-wall dark-wood shelves are full of beautiful, well-preserved books. The narrow Gothic windows offer a peaceful view of Merton's playing fields, and beyond them Christ Church Meadow stretches as far as the eye can see. Merton's library is quintessentially Oxfordian – a quiet, inviting place for people to blossom intellectually.

On the day of my visit, after a brief conversation about William Bell, Julian brought me the book with all the minutes of meetings of the Irvine Trust since 1924. He also gave me a book-rest made of foam and a thick purple thread, so I could mark the page I was reading. Finally he put in front of me a couple of flawlessly sharpened pencils and some paper, in case I wanted to take notes. Seeing the extreme care with which Julian treated everything, I asked him, half jokingly, half seriously, whether I should use gloves to turn the pages. He smiled kindly at me and said that it was not necessary.

Occupying only a page and a half of the book and in an almost illegible handwriting, the minutes of the 1948 meeting were written in a quite casual way. It just said, 'the annual meeting was held in Mr Cox's room in University College on Sunday, 23rd of May, 1948, at 9.30 am. There were present Bryant, Cox, Hull, and Thomas.' No further information about the members of the committee was provided. As was the custom in public schools and universities people referred to each other using their surnames only. Thirty-nine grants, totalling a little bit more than £200, were approved that day after examining forty-seven applications. The names of the recipients and the amount of money that each of them received was also listed.

I went through the records, wishing not to find William's name on them, as if, somehow, that could help him to avoid his fate. Unfortunately, there it was, and for a couple of seconds I felt as sad as I had the first time I saw his tombstone in Zermatt, a few weeks earlier. Beside the name appeared the amount he had received from the Fund – five pounds in total, a very modest sum even back in 1948, and according to my calculations, no more than £200 in today's money. A small note in the margin, written in pencil, informed the reader succinctly that 'Bell was killed in an accident on the Swiss ridge of the Matterhorn at the end of his holidays.' That was it.

With the support of Julian, I continued checking the archives in search of more documents, in the hope that William had filled in some kind of application form for the trustees where he described the duration, route and expected costs of their holidays as well as the peaks he intended to climb. We found nothing, not even the slightest reference to whatever plans William and his friends had. Finding more about the trip was still vital to me. Was climbing the Matterhorn the main purpose of the trip or was it just one of many mountains that they planned to assault? How had they travelled to Switzerland in 1948, when international travel was anything but easy? Where did they stay? How many people were in the group? Despite my best efforts, after the discovery of the obituaries I had found no new significant information. Somehow it was as if the world had entirely forgotten William, Ian and James: as if their story had vanished, devoured by the sands of time. That was a very distressing thought, and I knew that unless I got some answers my project of writing their story would be stalled for ever.

Of one thing I was certain, though: even if the five pounds of the Irvine grant did not represent a large sum of money, I could visualise William happily smiling on that Sunday of May 1948 when he got news that his application had been approved. It was almost as if I could share his happiness – but not entirely. After leaving Merton I realised why I had felt so heavy-hearted when I found William's name in the archives of the Irvine Trust. It was because I was aware of how the story ended. It was because I already knew that he was about to die on one of his beloved mountains – something that William couldn't have imagined that Sunday morning, more than sixty years earlier. That's how cruel life can be sometimes – we want to believe that we are in control of our own destiny, that we are the masters of our lives, without suspecting that destiny may have other plans in store for us.

I learned that lesson the hard way two months later, when I was in Mozambique for work. One night I got a terrible, sudden pain in the left side of my chest. The first reaction was to think that it was a heart attack. However, it did not make any sense – I do a lot of sport, have a healthy lifestyle and my blood pressure is quite good. Furthermore, I was too young, and had too many wonderful professional and personal projects to even consider that possibility. No, that could not be happening to me. When the doctor in the hospital told me that the problem seemed to be a 'horse-size' gastritis (as she graphically put it), which was causing a severe inflammation of some parts of my abdomen and with it a lot of pain, I felt an instant sense of relief. Yes, as I thought, a heart attack was something that could not happen to me. I was given some painkillers and for the next few hours everything went well. However, the next morning the pain returned, this time much more intensely, to a point where I could not even raise an arm, and on both sides of the chest as well as in the right side of my back. Clearly that was not gastritis. Urgently evacuated to England that afternoon, the doctors at the John Radcliffe Hospital in Oxford found a massive pulmonary embolism that had almost blocked both of my lungs. I was very lucky – had I stayed in Mozambique, without the right diagnosis, I would have certainly died there in less than 24-36 hours.

As Forrest Gump says, 'Life is like a box of chocolates. You never know what you're gonna get.'

6. The trickle turns into a flood

Surprise is the greatest gift that life can give us.
Boris Pasternak

One of the most extraordinary episodes of my quest for William, Ian and James happened while I was in Port Louis, the capital of Mauritius, at the end of September. Note the irony, as it's hard to imagine a more distant place from Switzerland than Mauritius. It is not just physical distance which separates both nations – almost 6,000 miles – but the fact that they are different in almost every single way. Switzerland is a rather conservative country, proud of its traditions and confident in its uniqueness, while Mauritius is an example of chameleonic capacity to embrace change. Mauritians are friendly and hospitable, as usually happens with people who live by the sea and are accustomed to the comings and goings of strangers. The Swiss, on the contrary, have the natural reserve of those who have lived for centuries voluntarily isolated in their remote valleys from the outside world. Switzerland is an immense ocean of mountains in the centre of Europe while Mauritius is just a minuscule pinch of ground at the corner of a vast ocean.

For me, however, these two very different places will always remain connected, thanks to the events of that weekend.

For those who have never been in Port Louis, it is fair to say that it is probably the least appealing part of the island. In fact, it has nothing to do with the images of sandy beaches and turquoise waters that are Mauritius' trademark. The city is built around its harbour – its true heart and the exit gate for the ships loaded with sugar cane, upon which the country's economy exclusively depended for centuries. Until the tourism boom in the 1980s,

65

money was always tight in Mauritius. You will not find any of the typical landmarks that epitomised the pretentious opulence enjoyed by other African and Caribbean towns in a not-so-distant colonial past. There are no swanky casinos or posh hotels built to accommodate the big landowners when they came into town. Big mansions, with classic colonnades and immaculate lawns, are not to be seen anywhere. Architecture is rather unrefined and tiny, ugly commercial buildings coexist with the modern towers that house big international banks currently using the island as a hub for their financial activities. The whole town is surprisingly small and most of the streets are narrow and dark.

For that reason, when my boss told me that I had to spend a few days working with the Central Bank of Mauritius, I decided to look for accommodation outside Port Louis. *Moin Choix,* a bed and breakfast on the outskirts of the town that claimed to be 'a home away from home', was my choice. Its website showed a tastefully decorated house perched on a mountainside, surrounded by sugar cane fields and dense forests, with magnificent views of the sea as well as of the rugged hills behind it. The reviews of former guests talked about a 'unique experience' and 'heaven on earth'. The place sounded too good to be true, but the moment I set foot there any reservations I had had quickly disappeared. The house was truly beautiful and, as promised, the views were splendid, especially from a veranda near the open-plan eating area. They were so 'to-die-for' that I immediately adopted the habit of sitting there every day to watch the sun disappear beyond the horizon, no matter how busy I was. The spectacle was an elaborate extravaganza of colours – the rosy clouds of the sunset merging with the dark blue of the ocean; of sensual aromas – the delicate fragrance of wet grass and the sweetness of sugar canes competing to fill the air with their scent; and of riveting sounds – the muezzins from the neighbouring mosques summoning the faithful to the evening prayers with the background of exotic birds making themselves comfortable in the trees surrounding the house before going to sleep.

It was one of those evenings while sitting on the veranda that I received a message that would turn the whole quest upside down. It was from Julian, Merton's archivist, from whom I had heard nothing since my visit to the college's library a week earlier. His email said:

> Dear Mateo,
>
> It was a pleasure to meet you last week; I am glad your visit was successful.
>
> I can now provide further information that I think will be of interest.
>
> Discussing your interest in Bell with our Fellow Librarian after your visit, it turns out that she has recently purchased some material by and about Bell for the library, because of his activities as a poet. The acquisition was so recent that the information has not yet got onto our catalogue and she had not had a chance to tell me about it. Rather than trying to describe the contents, I attach a scan of the bookseller's catalogue descriptions.
>
> I hope this information will be of interest; perhaps we will meet again soon!
>
> Regards,
>
> Julian

I was left speechless. Nobody at Merton had shown any interest in William for more than sixty years. Yet, exactly at the time when I was trying to gather information about his life, someone, in a completely unrelated way, had decided that it would be a good idea to buy whatever material they could find by and about him. It was an extraordinary coincidence.

The file that Julian sent to me listed all documents acquired by Merton. They included a copy of William's *Elegies*, his first published book; an autograph poem called 'On a dying boy'; a studio photograph of him; several letters and postcards written by William, as well as a letter sent after the accident by his father to Ian Davie, one of William's close friends. The list also contained the printed Order of Service for the memorial service for William, Ian and James, as well as a page from The Isis, a student magazine founded in the late nineteenth century, featuring 'the poetry of William Bell'. Merton had also acquired two other books by William: Twenty Sonnets and Mountains Beneath the Horizon, a collection of William's works published in 1950. Coincidentally, following an arduous search online, I had also bought one of the few existing copies of Mountains Beneath the Horizon, although it had not arrived before I left for Mauritius.

Additionally, the file contained a brief description of William, who was depicted as 'one of the lost poets of his generation, a close friend of John Heath-Stubbs and prime mover in Philip Larkin's career'. It also said of him that he was a poet for whom 'mountaineering seemed to be somehow a symbol of spiritual ascent'. The document also mentioned the names of other Oxford poets associated with William. Finally, it quoted an article from The Times of 28 July 1948, 'British climbers killed: 3,000 ft. fall on the Matterhorn', providing a brief account about the accident:

> The bodies of three Oxford undergraduates, found at the bottom of a 3,000 ft. precipice, were today being carried down the Matterhorn to Zermatt by a party of Swiss mountaineers. The three men, who set out on Sunday morning without a guide, had climbed about half way up the treacherous 14,705 ft. peak when one of them is believed to have slipped in the icy snow. It is believed the students were on their way down, because of the bad weather, when disaster overtook them.

Knowing that all those precious items were now available in

Merton was as frustrating as it was exciting, as I would have to wait at least another week for my return to the UK and the opportunity to take a look at them. However, it was not my intention to remain idle until that moment came. In fact, that very night I started looking for information about all the other names mentioned in the documents acquired by the college.

Philip Larkin didn't need an introduction – he was one of the major poets of post-war Britain and, despite his reputed deeply anti-social character, a favourite of the public as well. And William was described as a prime mover in his career! However, the names of the other poets – John Heath-Stubbs, Sidney Keyes, Drummond Allison and Keith Douglas – did not ring any bells. A search online revealed that all of them were students at Oxford during World War II, albeit not at the same time. Although it was unlikely that William knew all of them personally (some of them were already fighting in the war by the time he first came to Oxford), by editing the book *Poetry from Oxford in the Wartime*, which contained a selection of their poems, he had been the bond that had brought them together.

After Larkin, John Heath-Stubbs was the most celebrated member of the group; in 1973 he received the Queen's Medal for poetry and in 1988 he was awarded an OBE for his work. Almost blind from the age of three, his condition excluded him from participating in the war effort. That was a blessing in disguise, as many of his literary comrades died during the conflict and therefore never had the chance to see their talent recognised. Sidney Keyes, for example, was killed in action in Tunisia in 1943 while fighting with the British 7th Armoured Division, the Desert Rats. During combat, he continued writing, although none of these works survived. John Drummond Allison, another war poet, died in 1943 in Italy when leading an infantry platoon into the battle of Monte Cassino. Finally, Keith Douglas was killed by German mortar fire in Normandy in 1944, three days after D-Day, while his regiment was advancing from Bayeux.

"Another lost generation of poets," I thought, such as those who perished during the Great War: the likes of Wilfred Owen, Rupert Brooke, Isaac Rosenberg and Patrick Shaw-Stewart. At that moment, the verses of John McCrea's poem *In Flanders*, which he wrote during the Second Battle of Ypres in April-May 1915 – 'seventeen days of Hades!' as he put it – came to my mind:

> *In Flanders fields the poppies blow*
> *Between the crosses, row on row,*
> *That mark our place; and in the sky*
> *The larks, still bravely singing, fly*
> *Scarce heard amid the guns below.*
> *We are the Dead. Short days ago*
> *We lived, felt dawn, saw sunset glow,*
> *Loved and were loved, and now we lie*
> *In Flanders fields.*
> *Take up our quarrel with the foe:*
> *To you from failing hands we throw*
> *The torch; be yours to hold it high.*
> *If ye break faith with us who die*
> *We shall not sleep, though poppies grow*
> *In Flanders fields.*

In the words of the Colombian novelist Gabriel Garcia Marquez, author of *One Hundred Years of Solitude* and winner of the Nobel Prize for Literature in 1982, 'we only effectively die when we fully sink into the dark oblivion.' That night in Mauritius I went to sleep with the satisfaction of knowing that William was not entirely forgotten – not only did I remember him but, more importantly, now I knew that others at Merton did as well.

★

The next day was Saturday and I woke up quite early, a big a smile still drawn on my face as a result of the events of the previous evening. I went for a short run and after a quick shower I checked my email in case something important had arrived during the night. Nothing relevant, apparently. The only exception was a message sent by a certain Steve Broadbent, which was odd because I knew nobody of that name. I don't usually open emails from unknown senders, as there is too much spam and many viruses circulating on the net, but the title of the message, albeit containing only three words, was intriguing enough to make an exception. It said 'OUMC meet 1948'. When I opened it, I realised the message was not even for me – I was simply copied into it. The email's first words were 'Dear Mr McKean.'

McKean was Ian's surname and for a fraction of a second I thought it was some kind of sick joke. It was not. Like the moment I found the obituaries in the OUMC library, I had to take two or three deep breaths before continuing to read. The rest of the email said:

> *Thank you very much for taking the time to get in touch with us – I have copied your reply to the gentleman who was interested in this story, so that he may contact you if he wishes.*
>
> *Best regards*
>
> *Steve Broadbent*
>
> *President, Oxford Alpine Club*

Below there was another email and, as I scrolled down, I realised I was trembling with anticipation. In an enormous font, it said:

Dear Mr Broadbent,

Your enquiry about the OUMC event in Zermatt in 1948 has reached me by a devious path. As the brother of Ian McKean who was killed I was at the Hörnli hut on the day of the accident and being unwell overnight did not accompany the three who died.

I have no objection to being put in touch with your correspondent.

With good wishes

Donald C. McKean

Reading an email from Ian's brother was like a dream: so unreal that it was hard to believe, as if it was all just a trick of my imagination. To begin with, I didn't even know that Ian had a brother and, needless to say, I had not made any attempt to contact or locate him. Yet, he had somehow managed to find me. Even more bewildering was the fact that Donald McKean, who by now had to be in his mid-eighties, had also taken part in that ill-fated expedition to the Alps. Remarkably, he seemed to be happy to talk to me.

In many ways, the email was like some kind of miracle – a precious and unexpected gift; the sort of thing that you see in Frank Capra's movies such as *It's a Wonderful Life* or *Pocketful of Miracles*. Only it wasn't Christmas yet and I was certainly not on the snowy streets of Bedford Falls or New York City. It was an ordinary, sunny Saturday morning in September and I was in the middle of the Indian Ocean.

7. *What are the odds?*

There is no such thing as chance; and what seem to us merest accident springs from the deepest source of destiny.
Friedrich Schiller

Once I had recovered from the shock of reading Donald McKean's email, I started thinking about the steps that I should take next. On top of the list, obviously, was the task of writing to Steve Broadbent who, according to his email's signature, was the President of the Oxford Alpine Club. I had no clue as to how he had got involved in my quest for William, Ian and James, let alone how he had managed to locate Ian's brother. In any case, the least I could do was thank him for his role in this prodigy. The other pressing issue was preparing a good response for Donald McKean. My problem was that I didn't know what to say to him.

Contacting a librarian to request information about three students he or she was unfamiliar with was one thing. Getting in contact with a close relative of William, Ian or James, with all the emotional implications that this would surely have, was a completely different story.

In the case of Donald McKean, the situation was even more delicate as he was not *just* Ian's brother: Donald had been with William, Ian and James in the hut at the foot of the Matterhorn in 1948 and he was probably the last person who saw them alive. It was likely that he was also the first person who realised that something had gone terribly wrong, when night fell and his brother and his friends had not returned. I could imagine his increasing anguish in the hours before raising the alarm. Finally, he probably also had to identify the bodies once they were recovered.

All this made the prospect of talking to him simply overwhelming, even though such a long time had elapsed since the accident.

Of course, many times during the past weeks, I had wished to find a surviving member of the 1948 expedition, but had thought it extremely unlikely. In a way, it was like daydreaming about winning the lottery or like when, as a child, you fantasise about becoming a professional footballer – nothing more than wishful thinking: a fantasy. Well, to my immense surprise this time my wish had become real, and with it my journey had acquired an unexpected new dimension.

★

That very same day I started to get answers to some of my questions. For example, how Steve Broadbent had become involved in the quest was explained by Steve himself in an email later that morning. Ironically, it was I who had inadvertently triggered the whole process when, before travelling to Mauritius, I had contacted Tom Codrington, the OUMC Secretary, to get information about the trio of climbers. Unknown to me at the time was the fact that the OUMC and the Oxford Alpine Club were like twin brothers, with plenty of formal and informal links running between them. So, naturally, Tom had passed my request to Steve, who in turn had activated his vast network of contacts to trace Donald McKean.

Thus explained, it all seemed very simple, although I was certain that it could not have been so easy. Luck, necessarily, had to have played a major part: a point that Donald McKean seemed to confirm when he wrote that Steve's request had reached him by 'a devious path'.

After lunch, still not having a clear idea of what to tell Donald McKean, I went for a walk in the hope that it would help to put my thoughts in order: something that I desperately needed after the unexpected torrent of information that I had been flooded with over the last twelve hours. I headed downhill, towards the *Vallèe des Prêtres* (the 'Valley of the Priests'). In the middle of the valley there was a very modest hamlet with small but immaculate houses I passed by every day on my way to Port Louis. What had caught my attention about this place was that Hindus and Muslims seemed to live in complete harmony there. Just the day before, I had been thinking about James; as a British officer in India in the months preceding the partition, he probably had first-hand knowledge of the riots between the Hindu and Muslim communities that had seen between 200,000 and 500,000 people massacred in the Punjab region alone.

For that reason, when I arrived to the village, I was delighted to find a Ganesha shrine – the Hindu elephant god, with all its colours and flowers, its candles and incense sticks – side by side with a mosque, soberly painted in white and green. Hindu women dressed in saris were chit-chatting with their Muslim neighbours, most of them wearing hijabs. There was an atmosphere of peace and serenity in the air, in spite of the hubbub of the children who played in the main square. Tolerance is a factor that helps to explain the economic and social prosperity in Mauritius. Exactly like in Switzerland, where for centuries people of different origin (French, German and Italian) and religion (Catholics, Protestants and Calvinist, mainly) have lived together despite all their differences. This is notable because Europe's history has been shaped mostly by the notion of 'us versus them' – language and religion often being provided as the main excuses for killing those on the other side of the divide. Despite the craziness and butchery often unleashed around them by their European neighbours, Swiss people have managed to coexist with each other peacefully for centuries. Sitting on a bench under the shadow of a blossoming Flamboyant tree in the middle of the Valley of Priests, watching the Hindu and Muslim children playing together, I recall thinking that perhaps Switzerland and Mauritius were more alike than I had initially thought.

★

My therapeutic walk worked well, and by the time I was back in *Mon Choix* I had a clearer vision of what I wanted to tell Donald McKean, even though I had no idea what he had been told about my interest in his brother or how he had reacted to it. In any case, it was not difficult to imagine his surprise when he learned that someone, a total stranger, was interested in what had happened on the Matterhorn more than sixty years ago in 1948.

For me, the most important but also the most difficult thing was to put into words why I had felt so moved by his brother's tomb in Zermatt. In my response to him I mentioned the inscription on the bronze plaque – 'friends from Oxford killed together' and the profound impact it had on me. I also described the long silence after reading it, and how my wife held my hand tenderly as we stood there. I recall telling him how we read it again, two or three times more, still quite impressed by it.

I also described my findings in the library: the obituaries, and how they revealed the non-climbing side of his brother Ian, and also of William and James. I mentioned Ian's aspirations to build up a fair and egalitarian society and how much I respected him for that. I told Donald that 'what made William, Ian and James so special, in my eyes, was that they belonged to an extraordinary generation of Britons: those who lived through World War II, and were defined by values such as patriotism, idealism and generosity'.

Finally, I used the email to introduce myself properly; doing so was not just a matter of courtesy but a kind of *quid pro quo* obligation – it seemed wrong to be unearthing such sensitive information about a beloved member of his family without reciprocally letting him know about my own life. So in addition to explaining to him who I was, I also talked about my hobbies, my love for Britain and, of course, my passion for mountains.

I put all my heart into that email but I also wrote it with all the respect that such a special occasion deserved. For that reason I refrained from asking anything about the 1948 expedition, even though I was burning with a million questions about it. Likewise, I didn't suggest that we could eventually meet. Being pushy, even slightly pushy, was for me out of the question. So, by way of farewell, all I said was that I would be delighted to hear from him again.

A few minutes after writing to Mr McKean another email came into my in-box. It was from my wife, as a response to one in which I had explained to her all the events of the last twenty-four hours. Marian just wrote "WOW" in capital letters, with something like a hundred O's between the two W's followed by even more exclamation marks. Nothing summarises better my state of excitement and amazement during the whole day than her never-ending 'wow'.

By the time I went to sleep I was completely exhausted – too many emotions in such a short period of time. At that moment the last thing I expected was that Steve Broadbent would have another exciting surprise in store for me the following morning.

The message I received from him the next day said, "Mateo, here is another thread for you to follow if you wish. See forwarded message below from internationally acclaimed mountaineer Stephen Venables!" I scrolled down as fast as I could, my heart beating like a frantic drum. The message from Stephen Venables read:

> *Dear Steve,*
>
> *James Ogilvie was my father's cousin, and son of Sir Frederick Ogilvie (Director General of the BBC during the War, and subsequently Master of Jesus) and Lady Mary Ogilvie (later*

Imagine my surprise! Stephen Venables is a legend in mountaineering circles as he was the first British climber to ascend Mount Everest without using supplementary oxygen. In addition, he reached the highest summit in the world by opening a new route on the southeast side of the mountain, which made his achievement even more remarkable. However, in my eyes, that was nothing compared with the fact that he was a relative of James Ogilvie. "It's such a bloody small world", I thought.

The real icing on the cake was that James' brother, David, was still alive and, according to Stephen Venables, also keen to talk to me. That was something simply far beyond belief. In less than twenty-four hours I had been put in contact with the brothers of James and Ian. The whole thing was rather like attending an illusionist's show in which a magician kept pulling one rabbit after another out of a top hat – only that in this case the rabbits were absolutely real and the show was happening in front of my stunned and bewildered eyes.

I don't believe in determinism, nor any other kind of cause-effect relation to explain how events unfold in our lives. The future is never written. I don't believe in fate either. Life is what results when our free will and the chaotic environment that we inhabit get mixed together. We do create our own destiny. Yet, ridiculous as it may sound, that weekend in Mauritius I had the sense of being a puppet in the hands of I-don't-know-who for I-don't-know-what purpose. The rational side of my mind kept telling me that all these coincidences were just that: mere coincidences – but, so many? What were the odds that among the dozens of tombstones in Zermatt's cemetery I had laid eyes on this particular one? What were the odds of finding the obituaries in a journal written two years after the accident? What were the odds of Merton deciding to acquire all this material on William precisely now, after completely ignoring him for more than sixty years? What were the odds of locating the brothers of Ian and James, especially considering that I was not even looking for them? What were the odds that one of them, Donald McKean, had also participated in the Matterhorn expedition?

It is often said that lightning does not strike twice in the same place – apparently the chance of that happening is just one in 360 billion. However, sometimes odds can be beaten. I learnt it that weekend in Mauritius. These days were, for me, days of miracles and wonders.

8. Echoes from Scotland

The farther back you can look, the farther forward you can see.
Winston Churchill

The Polish journalist Ryszard Kapuscinski, acclaimed as the most brilliant and perceptive reporter of his time, writes in *Travels with Herodotus* that with every new town visited, with every new foreign word learnt, the traveller experiences small, almost imperceptible personal changes. Wherever you go becomes a part of you and the person who returns home is never the same as before departing. Knowing new people is in many ways like travelling, and those who you meet along your road become a part of your existence too. Since I first met William, Ian and James in Zermatt they had gone from being total strangers to becoming an important part of my life. In fact, in the last few weeks I had spent more time with them – thinking about them, looking for them, walking with them – than with anybody else.

Finding their obituaries had been the critical moment when they ceased to be just some names on a cold bronze plaque in a foreign cemetery and became actual people, with their own personalities, dreams and aspirations. Now, with the appearance of Ian and James's brothers, their presence was more tangible than ever. Knowing about Donald McKean and David Ogilvie also had the weird effect of blurring the boundaries of time. William, Ian and James ceased to be the inhabitants of a distant past and the whole quest stopped being restricted to the confines of 1948. In a way, it was as if the events in Mauritius had helped to build a bridge between the present and the past, and the presence of Donald McKean and David Ogilvie had brought their brothers back to life.

However, I was also concerned because I didn't know how that could affect them. One thing seemed certain, though – I was no longer the only person embarked on the journey initiated in the Mountaineers' Cemetery: Donald and David were now part of it too. My worst fear was that deeply buried, painful feelings could return to the surface, and alter their tranquillity. Upsetting Donald or David was definitely the last thing I wanted. Getting in contact with them would be a leap of faith. Having absolutely no idea what awaited me on the other side of the line was both intriguing and intimidating.

A couple of days earlier, a new message from Stephen Venables acted as a powerful reminder of the new dimension that my quest had acquired:

> *Dear Mateo,*
>
> *I have written to David, just to check that he is happy to hear from you. But I am sure that he will be.*
>
> *I remember James' mother showing me his diary from when he was doing National Service in India, shortly before he died. He seems to have been quite an idealist, very keen on Indian independence. David has since shown me a long article he wrote about a Scottish climbing trip with Bell and McKean, which I am sure you would find interesting.*
>
> *For Aunt Mary, I think James' death must have been a terrible blow, coming immediately after the death of her husband Freddie (he died young, probably because of gas injuries from the First World War).*
>
> *Stephen*

What Stephen's message was telling me was that William, Ian and James were not just someone's brothers, but also someone's sons. The email talked of the grief of a mother – not a random, unknown mother but his very own Aunt Mary's. The message talked about the tragedy of losing a son and a husband in the space of a few months; about feelings so painful and personal that they are impossible to comprehend unless you experience them first-hand.

★

The day I left Mauritius was sunny and bright. On my way to the airport, I gazed out of the taxi's windows at the endless sugar cane fields on both sides of the road. The breeze rocked them gently, like the waves of the sea on a quiet summer afternoon. By the time I arrived at the international departures terminal, I had another email blipping in my in-box. This time, from Donald McKean.

At the check-in desk the stewardess told me that my connecting flight to Johannesburg was delayed because of air traffic control problems in South Africa. For that reason, it was likely that I would have to wait at least three or four hours until I could board my flight. In other circumstances I would have mentally cursed for a while before accepting the inevitability of the delay, as well as my inability to do anything about it. But not that day. Instead, the disruption to my travel plans was a blessing in disguise: one that gave me the opportunity to read Donald's email calmly, and prepare a good response.

The waiting lounge was crowded with stranded passengers, almost all of them tourists, tanned red after endless hours of sunbathing on Mauritian beaches. There were some kids running here and there but the general atmosphere was quite gloomy. The prospect of abandoning paradise and returning home, combined with the frustration caused by the delays, created a sense of collective hangover, like in the morning after a big New Year's Eve party.

It was different for me. I had been working really hard in Mauritius for a week and returning home was a welcome prospect. Donald's email in my in-box was burning like pocket money in the hands of a little boy inside a sweet shop. After finding a seat in the quietest corner of the waiting room, I locked myself in a mental bubble, so focused that I didn't see or hear anything around me for a couple of hours. The text in Donald's email used the same large font as the email he had written to Steve Broadbent. This, I later found out, was caused by his eyesight problems.

Dear Mateo,

Many thanks for your message. My wife and I will be happy to support your project in any way we can. A new loss of eyesight means we need other means of communication. I suggest phone backed by a tape recorder or perhaps you and your wife could visit us in Edinburgh staying in our guest room, if this would help at some stage.

The material here may be daunting – we have my brother's diaries from school to army and Oxford in very obscure handwriting. They must include his year spent at Bletchley Park as a member of the ICorps.

AGNF was Tony Flew, a noisy member of the JCR at St Johns, my college, who I think became a Prof of Philosophy at Keele.

With good wishes, Donald McKean

After reading the message I raised my head and looked around; I could swear I was the only person smiling in the whole lounge. But I had good reasons for it – from the very moment when, a few days earlier, I had first written to Donald, I had tried not to have many expectations about he might say in reply, in case, for whatever reason, it was negative. Knowing that he was not only happy to help me but that he was also willing to meet me was extraordinary. He had even invited us to stay with them at their house, which was a very generous gesture from his side.

Of course, Marian and I agreed that staying in the McKeans' house was out of the question. Although we knew that his offer was totally sincere, we didn't want to be a nuisance to an elderly couple. We already felt guilty for invading their privacy, so the last thing we wanted to do was invade their personal space as well. In this regard, whenever we visit friends and relatives we always have in mind the words of Benjamin Franklin, one of the Founding Fathers of the United States: "Guests, like fish, smell after three days." So, after making our own arrangements for accommodation, I wrote to Donald to thank him for his kind email and nice proposal, and suggested that we would be able to travel to Edinburgh at the end of October.

Donald's email also contained several bits of extremely interesting information. First, he confirmed that Ian had served in Bletchley Park during the war, as a member of the Intelligence Corps. It was in Bletchley Park, also known as Station X, that the German *Enigma* and *Lorenz* codes were broken, effectively cracking the secrets of Nazi wartime communication. This, in turn, was crucial for the Allied victory. According to the military historian, Professor Richard Holmes, 'The work at Bletchley Park was utterly fundamental to the survival of Britain and to the triumph of the West. I'm not actually sure that I can think of very many other places where I could say something as unequivocal as that.' General Dwight D Eisenhower, the Supreme Commander of the Allied Forces in Europe, also said of Bletchley Park that the intelligence gathered there 'saved thousands of British and American lives and, in no small way, contributed to the speed with which the enemy was routed and eventually forced to surrender'. That Ian had been part of something so fundamentally important for the result of the war was indeed magnificent.

So I made a mental note – as soon as I returned to England I had to visit Bletchley Park.

The other interesting piece of information in the email was the identification of AGNF – the person who had written Ian's obituary in the OUMC journal – as Tony Flew. In my first email to Donald I had asked whether he knew who AGNF was, so I could contact him to talk about Ian. Tony Flew, as Donald had familiarly called him, turned out to be Antony Garrard Newton Flew, one of the most prominent British philosophers of the second part of the twentieth century. Sadly, I found out, he had passed away in 2010. The note I read about him in *The Guardian* mentioned that he was 'well known to a generation of students as an official atheist philosopher, much to the chagrin of his father, a Methodist minister, who is said to have prayed for him every day'. I read a few more press releases and all of them agreed that Antony Flew was a brilliant man, with an extraordinary intellectual capacity: a trait shared with the rest of William's poet friends.

Donald himself had had a distinguished professional life, becoming a Professor of Chemistry at the University of Edinburgh. It was clear that William, Ian and James had not only many personal and intellectual virtues but they were also surrounded by brilliant people: people who succeeded in life in one field or another. That day at Mauritius airport I was left wondering what they could have achieved if they had not died on the Matterhorn in 1948. At that moment the last sentence of their obituary, 'their death together is a loss not only to us who knew then, but to the future', made total sense to me.

Before getting on my plane, I read Donald's email once again and smiled when I spotted something in it that I had missed before – he described Tony Flew as 'noisy'. If, after all this time, he was able to remember this tiny detail, I was sure that the meeting with him would not only be extremely useful for my research but also quite fun.

9. *The mountains of your dreams*

If you can dream it, you can do it.
Walt Disney

After returning to the UK, I wrote to Tom Codrington, the OUMC secretary, to thank him for his role in getting me in contact with Donald and David. Also, I was keen to have a conversation with him about knife-edge ridges, rotten rocks and chest-deep snowfields on far-away mountains; about fear and vertigo; about the ecstasy of conquering a coveted summit and the despair of retreating in the face of an insurmountable obstacle on a treacherous wall. The list of topics I wanted to discuss with him was in fact endless – I was devouring every mountaineering book that fell into my hands, but the more I read the more questions I was left with.

In Mauritius, I had finished Thomas Hornbein's *The West Ridge*, the story of the 1963 American expedition to Everest, that intended to achieve what nobody else had done before: the traverse (ascending a peak by one route and coming down by another) of a 25,000 foot peak. On 1 May, after twelve hours of painfully slow progress on the daunting west ridge of the mountain, Hornbein and his partner, Willi Unsoeld, reached the summit at 9pm. That is, in pitch darkness. They spent the whole night in the open, huddled together, still well inside the 'Death Zone' – the area above 26,000 feet where the air is so thin that the human body begins to die. Hornbein's description of that night is of a brutal simplicity: "There was nothing. We hung suspended in a timeless void, pained by an intensive cold. Survival was hardly a conscious thought. Nothing to plan, nothing to push for, nothing to do but shiver and wait for the sunrise."

Hornbein and Unsoeld were completely worn out after weeks of intense physical activity preparing the assault on the mountain, after 'endless sleepless nights', after countless travails at altitudes incompatible with human life. Unsoeld was even suffering severe frostbite in his toes; nine of them had to be amputated once he came back. However, that night, both of them found the necessary inner strength to keep fighting and return to the camp alive. Where did their drive come from? That question resonated inside my head while reading of their hardships, but also with every new book about mountaineering that I wolfed down during those weeks. Naturally, the names of the climbers and mountains were different, but the resolution, the endurance beyond what is humanly possible, shown by all these men and women is always similar.

The question about climbers' mental and physical strength, about their no-surrender capacity, really puzzles me, because by normal standards it's fair to say that I'm quite a fit person. I even run a couple of trail ultra-marathons every year, so I know a thing or two about suffering and pain. Yet, what climbers are capable of doing in the most extreme circumstances is something that completely escapes my understanding.

While living in Bolivia, for example, I once went for a 15-mile high-altitude trek to the base camp that gives access to the Huayna Potosi peak (19,995 feet). It's no walk in the park, as most of the way is well above 16,500 feet. However, I was ten years younger and, having lived in La Paz for a while, I was well acclimatised to altitude. Yet, I have never been so depleted in my entire life – not even after completing a 50-mile race in Snowdonia, mostly at night, under non-stop rain. Weather conditions that day in Bolivia were perfect and the path was in a reasonably good state. However, for the last hour of the trek I had to make a conscious effort to keep walking – every step was like jumping a 10-foot wall while carrying a 220-pound rucksack. How on earth can climbers keep putting one foot in front of the other at an altitude of 25,000 feet? That day my body was yelling at me 'Stop, please, stop' every twenty seconds. I kept walking because I knew that at the end of the trail there was a car waiting to take me home. How do you keep moving when, after twelve or fourteen hours in the open, still the only prospect ahead of you is spending a night at minus 25 or 30 degrees Celsius, exposed to the screaming winds of the mountain, in a place where the mind wanders into strange and dark corners, while your fingers and toes are slowly dying?

I not only wanted to talk with Tom about physical and mental strength and Superman-like skills, but also about other ever-present elements in the climbing universe: elements such as success, ambition and selfishness, life and death. What do you do after stepping onto the top a mountain? What is your first reaction after the successful culmination of months, or even years of hard, thankless work preparing your next expedition? How do you feel after climbing the mountain of your dreams? Whenever I am in Chamonix and set eyes on the South-west Pillar of the Petit Dru, I wonder that. Considered for ages as the very essence of the unclimbable, it was conquered by Walter Bonatti in 1955, after five days of extraordinary solo climbing. The book in which he tells this story, and also takes a look back through his love-hate relationship with climbing, is *The Mountains of my Life*. Interestingly, his memoirs are exceptionally rich when it comes to technical details and solutions required to deal with problems. Yet, the book is quite shy when it talks about his emotions; about his fears and feelings; about his ambition to be recognised as one the best climbers in history. Bonatti's book is not an exception, though – very few mountaineering authors dare to offer a glimpse of the real people behind the public persona, as if the technical narrative they provide is a mask behind which everything else could, and should, be concealed.

This unwritten norm is broken by *The Ridge*, a documentary telling the story of the attempt to rescue Iñaki Ochoa de Olza – a Spanish climber who, on 20 May 2008, suffered a stroke on Annapurna's east ridge, well above 25,000 feet. The film, a beautiful rarity in the often inscrutable world of climbing, offers an intimate insight into the emotions and motivations of the more than a dozen elite climbers who risked their lives to try to save Iñaki.

The epicentre of the story is Annapurna's Camp 4 where, after suffering the stroke, Iñaki is in a desperate situation; he is in a semi-comatose state and cannot walk or move by himself. However, he is not alone. His climbing partner, the Romanian Horia Colibasanu, despite being himself in bad physical condition, has decided to stay with him. They have no medicine, no food and no fuel to melt snow, which is critical as the body quickly dehydrates at altitude. After making contact with base camp by radio to explain the gravity of their situation, a rescue attempt is organised. Among those who first respond to the call for help is the Swiss Ueli Steck, who was training in the proximity of Annapurna's south face. Despite his inadequate clothing and boots (all his high-altitude equipment was on another part of the mountain, ready for the moment when he decided to start his own attack on the summit), Steck starts to climb alone to take help to Iñaki. 'You have to be honest. Iñaki was really bad. You could say "there is no chance to help him" and take another beer, but this would have been wrong. You have to go up there and see what you can do. In this moment you have to believe that you can help him,' explains Steck, twice winner of the *Piolet d'Or* award which distinguishes the year's greatest ascents in terms of style, innovation and difficulty.

The Kazakh Denis Urubko and Canadian Don Bowie, who are both in Kathmandu, also respond immediately to the request for help. However, their helicopter trip to Annapurna's base camp is delayed by the extreme weather conditions. Carrying with them bottled oxygen and medicines, Urubko and Bowie start climbing Annapurna's south face twenty-four hours after Steck had spearheaded the rescue operation. For them, the ascent becomes a time trial, as they know that Iñaki won't be able to hold out much longer. "We knew that our chances were very small, almost insignificant, but we had to try. The climb was exhausting but in these circumstances you have to climb with your heart, not your legs," says Bowie. Both men almost died when avalanches fell twice from upper slopes, "We were like fish gasping for air," Urubko recalls. When they reach Camp 2, Alexey Bolotov, who was descending after having reached the summit a couple of days earlier, and despite suffering a pulmonary oedema himself, joins them. His decision is quite easy, he says, as he knows that Steck, Bowie and Urubko will need all the help they can get to take Iñaki down. "I did nothing heroic. We stayed together to try to survive and to help a friend," says Alexey.

When Steck finally reaches Iñaki and Horia, he finds that the Romanian is also in very bad condition, having been above 25,000 feet for almost a week. For the last two days, since Iñaki suffered the stroke, and while waiting for help to arrive, he has been melting ice in his mouth to keep Iñaki hydrated. Horia is also suffering the first symptoms of altitude sickness, and Steck is sure that he won't be able to descend by himself. After consulting with base camp, it is decided that Steck should try to take Horia down, as he has more chance than Iñaki of surviving. However, Horia refuses to leave his friend behind. "I am no hero. For me it was not an option to leave Iñaki there to die alone. Had I done it I would not be able to live with myself. So, morally, I had no option. I am sure he would have done exactly the same for me," says Horia. Only when Steck agrees to stay with Iñaki, does Horia accept that he should descend. The following day, and despite Steck's desperate efforts to keep him alive, Iñaki dies. Urubko, Bowie and Bolotov, with their precious charge of oxygen, are less than four hours away from Camp 4. "I turned to the ice wall and I screamed. I cried and screamed. I heard the wind inside my head," says Denis Urubko, recalling his reaction when he was told Iñaki had died. Nothing else could be done.

The heroism and generosity of those who participated in what is still considered as one of the most difficult rescue operations ever to take place in the Himalayas is even more striking as climbers are often accused of the opposite – of complete and utter selfishness: of putting their own goals ahead of everything and everybody else. Sometimes they are even accused of lack of basic human empathy.

The case of British mountaineer David Sharp, which made headlines in newspapers all over the world in 2006, is often used to illustrate this point. In May that year, David, while climbing solo on Everest's northeast ridge, began suffering the first symptoms of altitude sickness and took shelter on a rock overhang known as Green Boots Cave, ten feet off the main route to and from the summit. The place got its name because it is where the body of the green-booted Indian climber Tsewang Paljor, who died there ten years earlier, rests for ever. Completely immobile, although lucid at times, David slowly died over many long hours. During that time, roughly forty climbers passed him on their way to the top but no one stopped to render aid. 'My name is David Sharp and I am with Asian Trekking', it is reported that he said to some of those groups. David's chances of being rescued, like in the case of Iñaki, were almost none, as he could not walk without help. However, had he received some aid when he began to feel sick, he perhaps could have recovered enough to try to descend by himself. Twelve elite climbers responded to the call to help Iñaki – some of them even came from such distant parts of Nepal as Kathmandu, more than 180 miles away. However, none of the climbers ascending Everest that day stopped to check David's state, although he was dying barely ten feet from them.

Unfortunately, David's story is not an exception. The death of an Indian climber in 1992, left to die alone only ninety feet away from the safety of tents on the south col of Everest, where dozens of other climbers were sleeping, was used by Joe Simpson in *Dark Shadows Falling* to explore the ethics of climbing.

Many of those who were in the tents heard him screaming, but they didn't go out to hold the dying man. No one acknowledged his last despairing movement, knelt by him and had the humanity to hug him. He died alone as his fate was discussed earnestly in a bizarre radio call.

Heroes or villains? This is a question that I have asked myself many times during this quest.

★

The day I met Tom Codrington he came accompanied by two friends from the OUMC – Peter Hill and Robert King, who had climbed the Matterhorn in 2009. I soon realised that in many respects they were typical Oxbridge students – articulate, intelligent and confident. They also seemed to be extremely knowledgeable about mountains. However, I was pleased to discover that they were also down-to-earth young men, without any trace of the arrogance or the theatrical attitudes that is the trademark of some of their peers. Our lunch at the Old Tom, a traditional British pub on St Aldate's where, ironically, you can eat what is probably the best Thai food in town, was not only very pleasant, but enlightening too, as we discussed plenty of things about climbing over the three hours or so that we spent together.

One of the most interesting parts of the conversation revolved around the thin line separating mountaineering from climbing – words that for a layman like me sound indistinguishable, but which are really not. Essentially, mountaineering is all about getting to the top of a mountain, which requires in many cases rock and/ or ice climbing skills. That means that most mountaineers are also climbers to some degree or other. However, the opposite – that all climbers are mountaineers – is not true, as climbing can also be practised indoors, by the sea (cliff-climbing), or even among buildings – known as buildering. Alain Robert, the so-called 'French Spiderman', regarded by many as the greatest of all builderers, has never climbed a mountain. However, the list of his feats – completed using no climbing equipment except for a small bag of chalk – is exceptional, and includes ascents of the Empire State Building in New York City (1,453 feet), the Jin Mao Tower in Shanghai (1,381 feet), Taipei 101 in Taiwan (1,670 feet), and each of the Petronas Towers in Kuala Lumpur, Malaysia (1,483 feet).

Like many modern sports, the idea of climbing a building was born in Britain's public schools during the nineteenth century. The first book about roof-climbing, Geoffrey Young's *The Roof-Climbers' Guide to Trinity*, was published in 1895. Considered as the greatest English mountaineer of his era, Young was, like William Bell, a poet; he won the Chancellor's Medal for English Verse two years in a row while studying at Cambridge. As a climber, he made several new and difficult ascents in the Alps before World War I, including routes on the Breithorn, on the west face of the Weisshorn and a dangerous and rarely repeated route on the south face of the Täschhorn. During the war, while serving as an ambulance driver on Italy's Isonzo Front in August 1917, he lost his leg after being hit by an Austrian shell. Despite this, he continued climbing for a number of years using a specially designed artificial leg. He even climbed the Matterhorn in 1928. According to Wade Davies, Young was also George Mallory's mentor and the main reason that he received an invitation to join the Everest expeditions.

However, my favourite book on buildering is not Young's but the anonymous *The Night Climbers of Cambridge*, a high-spirited account of nocturnal climbing activities on some of the most iconic buildings in Cambridge. The book, written in 1937 by members of a secret society of university students, contains not only some wonderful pictures and detailed descriptions of the routes to climb buildings like St John's chapel, the Old Library and Trinity College, but it also blatantly proclaims the reasons to do it – 'official disapproval is the sap which gives roof-climbing its sweetness.'

During our lunch, Tom unequivocally defined himself as a climber. For him, climbing was basically a problem-solving activity: a mental exercise to find technical solutions to problems on rock. He even argued that climbing requires more intellectual capacity than physical strength, an idea that I found not only quite unusual but provocative as well. At home, later that night, I found that Tom was not the only one defending that thesis – in 1989, the English poet Al Alvarez said in his book *Feeding the Rat: a Climber's Life on the Edge* that 'climbing is a paradoxically intellectual pastime, during which you have to think with your body'.

That reminded me of a day, a few years ago, in the Peak District, where I was hill walking. I stopped to watch the progress of a climber on Stanage Edge; he seemed to be in his early twenties and, like a salamander of vivid colours, his legs and arms were completely stretched out on the wall. Fifteen or so feet below, a female friend was belaying him – a safety measure to stop him from falling very far. In my ignorance, I probably had the hope of seeing him doing something spectacular, as if I was watching a free training session of the *Cirque du Soleil*. Nothing was further from reality. To my disappointment he barely did anything in the more than ten minutes that I stood there. He cautiously tested one hold here and there, he stretched his arms to check whether he could reach this or that place; that was all. Well, that, and a lot of talking too – they spent most of the time discussing the convenience of moving one leg 15 centimetres to his right. In many ways, it was like watching a chess game against the wall, with the two climbers discussing all the possibilities that would follow from making a move with one of their pawns.

Tom also talked at length about his recent trip to Kyrgyzstan, where he had spent ten days hanging on a 4,000 foot wall. The climb, he said, was entirely on rock. "I tend to avoid ice and snow as they distort the nature of the challenge before you, making it more uncertain and capricious. Dry rock, on the other hand, is more predictable; you know better what set of solutions need to be applied." Tom described his climb methodically, as if he were a scientist explaining the progress of a physics experiment in a laboratory. In my notes, I wrote that he depicted climbing challenges as equations that needed to be solved. When I mentioned this to him, he agreed: "In fact, most of the people in our climbing club who define themselves as climbers are science students, while mountaineers are more likely to be arts students."

At that point in the conversation, I mentioned the name of the American John Gill, who probably epitomises better than anybody else the concept of climber-cum-scientist. In Krakauer's *Eiger Dreams*, Gill is described as a living legend: someone who in the mountaineering 'Hall of Fame' would occupy a place of honour alongside Sir Edmund Hillary, Hermann Buhl, Walter Bonatti or Reinhold Messner. In other words, a great among the greatest of all time. In his case there is a funny twist, though. 'Customarily, a person gains entry in the mythology of this sport through death-defying deeds in the Himalayas, Alaska or the Alps. Gill's reputation, though, rests entirely on ascending nothing bigger than thirty-foot boulders,' writes Krakauer. Not surprisingly, until his retirement in 2000 John Gill was a Professor of Mathematics at the University of Southern Colorado, where he authored more than thirty papers on the analytic theory of continued fractions.

In preparation for the meeting, I had gathered some quotes from famous climbers and mountaineers. Basically, I wanted to see how Tom and his companions reacted to them. A couple of them belonged to Gill. One said, 'boulder climbing and mathematics are intrinsically similar, as both activities are based on pattern recognition', while the other provocatively stated that 'climbing is less a sport than an activity with metaphysical, mystical, and philosophical overtones'. After reading them, I noticed that Rob and Peter had a cheeky smile on their faces. When I asked them what they thought about Gill's words, Rob, in a polite, soft way, said, "Kind of gibberish, isn't it?"

That comment came as no surprise, as Rob and Peter, unlike Tom, had unequivocally defined themselves as mountaineers. "Mountaineering," Rob said, "involves much more than simply going from A to B. It may sound ridiculously obvious, but you cannot practise mountaineering unless you are on a mountain. So everything about that mountain, its beauty and that of the other peaks around, the bond you develop with it, forged during the long hours preparing the assault, and so on, become part of the experience." Peter supported this idea, adding, "Mountaineering is a holistic activity that brings many things together, including weather, logistics, and a real sense of danger." For that reason, he concluded, it was more 'authentic' than just climbing.

Listening to Tom, I made a mental note that climbing seemed to be a sort of self-contained activity, an end in itself – it seemed evident that a climber could be perfectly happy in the middle of a wasteland, provided he had some exciting challenge to decrypt. For Tom, mountains were more like accessories, while for Rob and Peter they were their alpha and omega, the beginning and end of everything they did. At this point, I read them a quote from Charles Evans who, in his valedictory address as President of the Alpine Club in 1970, had said, "Interest seems to have moved towards prowess and technique and away from the setting, away from the mountains themselves." The three of them agreed that this was probably the case.

★

Although the distinction between climbing and mountaineering was less clear in 1948 than today, I could not help but wonder how William, Ian and James would have defined themselves. Interestingly, their obituaries offered some clues in such respect. William's, for example, explained that 'he liked routes rather than problems', in what was a clear indication that his love for mountains was more important than climbing problem-solving. Tom's comment about the way science and arts students usually see themselves also fit with what I knew about the three boys. Both Ian and James were reading Classics at Balliol. In the case of William, he started reading Physics when he first came to Oxford in 1942 but by the time he returned from the war in 1946, he had changed his mind and began reading English instead. Perhaps, somehow, the war affected the way he saw life and the world and that in turn affected the way he perceived mountains. In Ian's obituary, Tony Flew said of him, 'Ian was never, and would never have become, technically outstanding, but he had every quality which really matters – good sense, endurance, cheerfulness and a passion for mountains.' Like William, Ian seemed to be a mountaineer at heart, rather than a climber, with a deep love for mountains and nature as his main driving force.

Back at home that night, I wrote in pencil at the end of James's obituary: "mountaineering is the search for your own soul" followed by a big question mark. At this point I remembered the words of George Mallory; while touring the United States to raise funds for the 1924 expedition to Mount Everest, he was asked why he wanted to climb it. "Because it's there," was supposedly his reply.

Even though mountaineers are well known for being spare with words, I always thought that this was an odd, shallow answer. Perhaps for Mallory the main motivation to climb Everest had to do more with duty, glory and honour than with the mountain itself. Or perhaps, after being on the road for some time, he was just tired and responded to that question with the first thing that crossed his mind. Some authors even suggest that Mallory never said it, and that the most famous three words in mountaineering were in fact the product of the imagination of a New York reporter. Who knows? Of one thing I was pretty certain, if someone had asked William Bell, Ian McKean and James Ogilvie why they decided to climb the Matterhorn, I don't think that any of them would have just replied "because it is there".

10. On the slopes of the Matterhorn

The other side of every fear is freedom.
Marilyn Ferguson

"A proud and lofty obelisk of living rock which seems to have been carved with a chisel." This is how Horace-Bénédict de Saussure, the Swiss aristocrat, scientist and Alpine traveller, who is often considered the founder of Alpinism, described the Matterhorn in 1789. Almost a century later, Albert Mummery, a Briton seen by many at that time as one of the finest climbers in the world, also wrote about his first impressions of the Matterhorn: "I remember, as if it was yesterday, my first sight of the great mountain. It was shining in all the calm majesty of a September moon, and, in the stillness of an autumn night, it seemed the very embodiment of mystery and a fitting dwelling place for the spirits with which old legends people its stone-swept slopes."

In the initial stages of my journey I extensively read what others, mostly travellers from the eighteenth century and climbers from the Golden Age of Alpinism, had written about the Matterhorn. Their thoughts and comments came to add a lyrical dimension to my own observations of the mountain, which I had patiently gathered during endless hours spent examining its ridges and faces from different places in the vicinity of Zermatt. Yet, it was not enough – I was eager to talk to people who had actually been on its slopes, embraced its rocks, and felt its terrifying yet riveting pulse. For that reason, a couple of days after my first encounter with Rob and Peter, I met them again, this time to talk almost exclusively about the Matterhorn. In particular, I was interested in their experience on the Hörnli Ridge – the route they followed during their successful ascent in 2009, which had also been used by William, Ian and James almost sixty years before.

However, there were other topics that I very much wanted to cover that day, like how they managed to cope mentally with the risks that climbing involved. Did they ever think about the possibility of having a serious accident or even dying on this or that mountain? Today, more accurate weather reports, better information about routes and climbing conditions, and the higher levels of safety provided by modern materials have certainly reduced the risks that mountaineers face. Yet, more people than ever die on mountains. Is this just a matter of probability – there are more people climbing hence the likelihood of fatal accidents is also higher – or is our perception of risk somehow different from that of our grandfathers and, as a result, we are more prone today to take chances that in hindsight are not such a good idea?

Intuitively, It could be argued that the latter is true. Today we live as if we were completely immune to death or disease, as if we were indestructible, immortals. Car accidents, for example, always happen to others, who undoubtedly are more stupid and worse drivers than we are. We behave as if everything in our lives is solid and durable, not realising – or preferring not to – that the opposite is true: that all that surrounds us is ephemeral. Perhaps it is human nature to ignore the fact that it may just take a small piece of food getting stuck in the upper airway, or a drunken driver coming in the opposite direction, or a small virus, to put an end to all that we have patiently built up for years. Permanently.

Dave Freeman knew this very well. In his book *100 Things to Do Before You Die* he wrote, "life is a short journey. Make sure you fill it with the most fun and visit the coolest places on earth before you pack those bags for the very last time." His recommendations ranged from attending the Oscars ceremony, or watching the Monarch Butterfly migration in Mexico, to more obscure options such as taking a voodoo pilgrimage. Free of financial worries after the success of his book, Dave's main goal in his life was to complete the list. However, in 2008, having worked his way through half of it, including running with bulls in Pamplona, Spain, and 'land-diving' in Vanuatu, he fell over at his home, hitting his head on a coffee table. He died instantly.

Death is a big taboo nowadays – probably much more than ever before in human history. However, the interesting thing about death is that we don't entirely reject it. On the contrary, death is all around us. In seconds, with a simple click on your computer, you may see a graphic account of yesterday's horror in the Middle East or pictures of the victims of another school shooting in the US. We cope with the idea of death either by trivialising it (action movies and violent video-games are a good example) or simply denying that it has anything to do with us. Yes, death is all around us, but it is always someone else's death; we are too young, or too handsome, or too successful to even think for a minute that any day, any single day, could be our last.

However, it was not like that in 1948. In an era when medicine was not so advanced, and diseases which are easily treatable today could be fatal, sickness and death were seen as part of the natural cycle of life. Additionally, World War II had ended barely three years before. During the conflict more than 380,000 British soldiers as well as 70,000 civilians had been killed – almost one per cent of the total population of the country. By the end of the war in 1945 more than 3.5 million men had served in the army. For all of them, as well as for their families and the hundreds of thousands of civilians affected by the Blitz, death was a very real possibility: something that could hit them at any time, any day.

Was the perception that William, Ian and James had of the perils of mountaineering somehow modified by the war? During this entire quest, and when confronted by questions like this, I always tried to put myself in their shoes – in this case, in James's. As a trooper with the Scots Greys in Holland in 1944, he participated in arduous battles to defend 'Hell's Highway', the road connecting Eindhoven and Nijmegen, from the German counterattacks. In the words of the American historian Leonard Rapport, the fighting to hold the Allied position was almost as fierce as during D-Day and the liberation of Normandy. 'The enemy's cutting of the road did not mean simply his walking across a piece of asphalt. It meant clogging the road for its entire length with vehicles that suddenly had nowhere to go. For the men of the British 1st Airborne Division at Nijmegen and Arnhem, cutting the road was like severing an artery.' During the campaign, which ranged from late September to December, the Allied forces experienced the misery of being trapped for weeks inside frozen, muddy foxholes, while enduring endless, overwhelming artillery barrages. The rate of casualties sustained by the Scots Greys was very high. Under these circumstances, I have no doubt that James saw many of his comrades injured or killed.

Compared to that, being in the Alps that summer of 1948 had to be for him, as well as for William and Ian, like enjoying a little piece of Heaven on Earth. They came from Britain, a country half-destroyed and half-starved, still suffering the ravages of war. By contrast, Switzerland was unscathed, food was plentiful, and, judging by the pictures in François Gos's book *Zermatt and its Valley*, published some years before the war, the scenery surrounding them could not be more idyllic. In the Garden of Eden that the Alps were, I am certain that the three young students from Oxford had reason to feel nothing but jubilant. They had survived a war, the pressure of the academic year back at the university was left behind for good, and they had the prospect of bright lives ahead of them. Above all, they were doing what they loved most – climbing mountains. What else could they ask for? In this state of mind, I cannot imagine that thoughts of disaster crossed their minds, even for a single moment, that Sunday in July when they started on their way up on the Matterhorn. Of course, they would have been aware of the risks that the climb involved and I am sure that they took them very seriously. However, precisely because they knew how fragile life could be, I am certain that it was love and gratitude for being alive, rather than apprehension or fear, that filled their hearts that morning.

★

With all this background, it was natural that I asked Peter and Rob whether they felt any fear while climbing the Matterhorn. "No," was their unequivocal answer. "Training helps you not only to improve your technical skills but also to learn how to deal with fear so you can put it to the back of your mind," Peter said.

"When you are up there, it's like you set yourself in a kind of auto-pilot mode. You simply stop thinking and the only thing that occupies your mind is the rock ahead of you. And then, somehow, you just follow your instincts," added Rob.

I knew first-hand what they were talking about. Earlier that year, my wife's present for my birthday had been a skydiving course at Netheravon, an airfield in the middle of Salisbury Plain. Over a weekend, I attended the methodical training course provided by parachute instructors from the army. We were taught how to fly, how to orientate ourselves while up in the sky, and how to land without breaking our necks. More importantly, for hours, again and again, we practised how to open the emergency parachute in case the principal one experienced some kind of malfunction. The goal was to increase our confidence in what we were about to do. Still, the night before the big solo jump I was scared to death. To my surprise, though, when the big moment came the following day, I was 100 per cent ready. In fact, I was so focused that I barely remember anything of it. Jumping from a perfectly functioning plane is a crazy thing to do. However, when I stepped onto the door of the plane and pulled myself out, in my head there was no room for fear, doubts or for anything else – I was indeed in auto-pilot mode and I knew exactly what I had to do to have a smooth ride.

The idea of emptying your head while climbing is similar to the distinction between explicit and implicit learning that Malcolm Gladwell uses in his book *What the Dog Saw and Other Adventures*, to explain why some people deal with pressure better than others: "when you are first taught something – say, how to hit a backhand or an overhead forehand in tennis – you think it through in a very deliberate, mechanical manner. That is explicit learning. But as you get better, the implicit system takes over: you start to hit a backhand fluidly, without thinking. In the end, you don't really notice what your hand is doing at all." However, under certain conditions, such as stress, the explicit system may take over again. It is at these times that you start over-thinking. If that happens, you may choke, and with the choking comes the panic and almost inevitable failure. Training, as Peter suggested, is the key to strengthening your implicit system; the more you train, the more easily you do something automatically, without having to think about it. Climbing, then, becomes something as naturally ingrained as walking or talking.

However, no matter how much you train, the danger that surrounds climbing never fades away completely; it follows you everywhere, like your own shadow. As Bernadette McDonald, the author of *Freedom Climbers*, says, 'the possibility of death is always present, as real for experienced climbers as for novices. Every alpinist knows this and all are forced to deal with this knowledge in their own way.' William knew it too. In 1947, on his first trip to the Alps with the OUMC, one of the members of the Geneva University Club, 'a very pleasant but incautious guy', with whom they were climbing, died in Arolla after the rope holding him broke and he fell down a 1000-foot precipice.

Danger, for climbers, is like a wild beast that they try again and again to tame, rather than to avoid or escape from. In a world where amputated toes are sometimes displayed as badges of honour, danger constitutes, in the words of Joe Simpson, 'the real essence of mountaineering: that strange mixture of fear and excitement, the addition of apprehension and anticipation without which mountaineering would simply be another sport'.

Along the same line of thinking, *The Night Climbers of Cambridge* proclaims:

> *A climber is as a man standing on the edge of an abyss. The chance of falling over or of the ground crumbling beneath his feet is negligible, yet his very closeness to the edge makes him think. He cannot but visualize what would happen if he stepped forward, and realizes with a shock of what very small significance it would be. The sun would still be shining, and the waterfall would still be roaring below. And suddenly he realizes what a friendly fellow the sun is, what vividness there is in the green around him. Thus, there is a kind of fear which is very closely akin to love, and this is the fear which the climber enjoys.*

Thus, for climbers, life and death are like indivisible parts of the same coin, with one illuminating the other. Up there, in the heights, life without death makes no sense. Most of us – people who look up at mountains from the valleys but never dare look out from their tops – spend most of our lives constructing solid walls behind which we hope to find security, without realising how fragile their foundations often are. Climbers know that any sense of permanence in life is completely fake: an illusion no more durable than a rainbow at the end of a rainy afternoon. And they know it from experience – most of those who climb mountains, at one time or another, have thought that their time has finally come, convinced that day would be the one from which they would not return home alive. All of them, elite and amateur climbers alike, have friends or partners, or friends of friends, who have died in the mountains. They know that it is dangerous, and yet, as Joe Simpson explains, 'if death were not ever present, many would not be drawn to it. Death, in a paradoxical way, validates the life-affirming nature of the game played.'

★

I asked Rob and Peter what their most vivid recollection about the Matterhorn was. I expected them to mention the imposing scenery or how special it was to reach the top of such a legendary mountain. Instead, they talked about how long and tiresome the climb was. Neither how beautiful it was nor how excited they were, just how long it was – more than six hours to reach the summit and a further seven in descent. The descent, they recalled, was particularly strenuous, so you had to be completely focused all the way down. "It was quite taxing for everybody in the group but in particular for the person leading it, because of the extra responsibility that entails", Peter mentioned. "It is during the descent when, because of the accumulated fatigue, it is easier to make a mistake," they reminded me. I could not agree more. Statistics stubbornly show that most fatal accidents on mountains occur while descending. Quite often climbers are so desperate to reach the summit that they forget that the real objective is not that in itself, but to do so and return home safely. As a result of this fixation – this summit fever, as some call it – one of the golden safety rules in climbing is often ignored: the one that says that you should turn back if you have not reached the summit at a particular predetermined time, in order to save enough energy for the descent.

Rob and Peter also said, to my surprise, that they had not enjoyed the climb at all. "The whole mountain is crowded, which in some sections is quite dangerous as rocks accidentally knocked off by climbers above you fall upon those below. Also, bottlenecks are formed in some areas, as there are many people waiting to use the fixed ropes, so you have to wait for a long time for your turn." They also said that the Matterhorn was much more beautiful from below than from the top. So, why did they do it? According to them, because it is difficult to escape from its mystique: "You are there, and you think 'how am I going to come back home without climbing the Matterhorn?' So even though you know that it's not going to be a great experience, you still do it." However, they made clear that they enjoyed climbing other peaks, such as the Grünhorn, or the Zinalrothorn, much more than the Matterhorn: mountains less congested, where you could be more in contact with your surroundings, rather than feeling like you were in London's Oxford Street on Boxing Day.

Like William, Ian and James in 1948, Rob and Peter had decided to climb the Matterhorn without seeking the assistance of a professional guide, even though this puts the person leading the group under greater pressure, both mentally and physically. "Mentally because you know that the safety of your colleagues is in your hands; and physically because finding and leading the route demands a bigger effort from your body", said Rob. Despite being aware of that, they always climb guideless because, in their opinion, making decisions is a critical part of the thrill of mountaineering, "If you just limit yourself to following a guide, you are not making decisions; it is as if you were not actually doing the climbing", Peter explained.

As a climber you need to be aware of your limitations – a basic common-sense concept that the commercialisation of mountaineering is helping to blur. That is why, many climbers agree, so many accidents happen these days. In some ways, mountains have become an entertainment ground for wannabes: people who wear crampons for the first time in their lives when they arrive at base camp on a 25,000 foot mountain; people who can afford to pay the top money asked by commercial firms, and who in turn demand to be taken to the summit no matter what. People who believe that the money they are paying can buy them a safe ascent of any summit. Thus, in the last few years, the number of enterprises peddling guided ascents of the notorious Seven Summits (the challenge consisting in climbing the highest peak on each of the continents plus Antarctica) has multiplied at an astonishing rate. As a result, during the climbing season, places like Everest are so crowded that dangerous queues form at points along the routes. This was identified as the main reason for the 1996 disaster on Mount Everest, when eight people died during summit attempts. For Tom and Pete, the answer to that problem is easy, 'If you need a guide to climb a mountain, then you need to ask yourself whether you should be there in the first place'.

Before leaving, we had a good laugh when I showed them another quote from *The Night Climbers of Cambridge*, this time about what it is like to reach the summit of a mountain or the highest pinnacle of a church:

> *Perhaps the first feeling is one of disappointment. The ambition of which you have been dreaming for weeks, or even months, is finished, and you must find another to replace it. You have been dreaming, glorying in the thought of it, and now in a few drab moments after the thrill of endeavour you are in the throes of success. But the exaltation will come later. When all is over, you will enjoy facing your bed-maker's cross-examination, replying to her queries by a bland look of innocence and a rather fatuous grin. You will bounce about with tremendous satisfaction, and feel more pleasure in living than you have ever known. The exaltation resulting from a difficult climb lasts for about three days, and during that time you will feel the devil of a fellow.*

"That's exactly it," they replied with broad smiles on their faces.

We talked about many other things that day: about why they started climbing in the first place but also about the strength of the new materials for ropes; about belay devices and dreams; about exposed ridges and impossible acrobatics on a wall. We also talked about the death of a dear friend of theirs, Lydia Press, a couple of years earlier, on the north face of the Tour Rond, in the Mont Blanc massif. Lydia, a former president of the OUMC, had graduated in environmental geochemistry from St Peter's and at the time of her death was studying for a Masters in environmental science in Budapest. At 24, like William, Ian and James, she had everything going for her in life. And like them, she loved mountains with all her heart.

★

When we parted ways later in the afternoon, I recall thinking how enjoyable the conversations with Tom and Pete had been. I not only learnt a lot about mountaineering – the kind of profound insights that are rarely explained in books – but also about human nature, about the desires and fears that live inside all of us but that only surface in extreme circumstances, like those that climbers so often have to deal with.

Listening to Tom and Pete helped me to understand William, Ian and James much better as well. Separated as they were by more than sixty years, all of them, the young men from 1948 and the twenty-first century climbers with whom I had spent the last few hours, shared not only the indomitable drive of youth, but were also united by the same passion. Somehow, they were intimately related to each other; all of them were members of the brotherhood of mountains.

11. A face-to-face with William

Unless we remember, we cannot understand.
E. M. Forster

In addition to meeting Tom, Peter and Robert, my other priority after returning to the UK was reading William's *Mountains Beneath the Horizon*. Before travelling to Mauritius, and after an arduous search, I had found it on an online site that specialised in rare and antique books. It was their last copy for sale. However, by the time I had to leave it had not yet been delivered. As a result, the only thing that I knew about it was what Marian had mischievously told me by email: "It's cool", she had said referring to the book, without adding anything else. I guess that it was my well-deserved retribution for all the times that, whilst abroad, I had teased her by saying that I had bought a gift for her only to refuse to provide further details about it.

The book was waiting for me when I arrived back home, early in October. It was indeed very beautiful, or so I thought, with the kind of elusive exquisiteness that only a few unique objects are entitled to possess, like a collection of old tin soldiers, or some delicate coral necklace. Tightly bound, it had bright yellow boards with gilt lettering, slightly darker in the corners. It was protected by a dust jacket, and it seemed to be in pretty good condition for a second-hand, sixty-year-old book. The title was in a black font, surrounded by a small floral ornament in red ink. Below it could be read 'Poems by William Bell, edited with an introduction by John Heath-Stubbs'. It had been published originally by Faber and Faber, a publisher that specialised in poetry. T. S. Eliot was Faber's Director of Publishing from 1925 until his death in 1965 so it was not unlikely that one of the greatest English-language poets of the twentieth century had read William's poems and approved their publication.

I opened it with extreme care and I smelled it, as I always do when I get a new book. For a copy published in 1950 – the year during which the war in Korea started and *The Archers* was first premiered by the BBC – it still retained a strong smell of leather, like a pair of good shoes that had been recently polished with beeswax. The touch of its pages was firm but also soft at the same time. Somehow, it felt like holding a very fragile creature, a little seahorse or a duckling, in my hands. And yet, in an entrancing way, the book radiated fortitude. I recall staring at it and wondering how many people would have lovingly opened it before I did it; how many people read it in its more than half-a-century of life; what long road it would have travelled before finally landing in my house.

The book contained a full-page portrait of William. It was only then that I realised I had never seen a picture of him. In fact, I did not have a clue about his looks or physical appearance. That was odd because William, together with Ian and James, had been my loyal companion for the last two months, his name and parts of his life being now as familiar to me as those of an old friend. Yet, until that moment, I wouldn't have been able to recognise him if he stood in front of me. Looking at his picture I experienced the same sense of amazement and strangeness that the bride and groom in an arranged marriage must feel when they come face to face with each other for the first time on their wedding day.

In the picture, clearly a studio portrait, William had a gentle and boyish look. His frank, rounded face was without a trace of a beard or facial hair. He was wearing a green or blue shirt and a tie of a similar colour. His clothes had the drab aspect of a military uniform, and the extremely neat side-parted hairstyle helped to accentuate the formality of the look. However, the young man in front of me also had a wide smile on his face, with a sort of amused look in his cheeky, bluish-almond eyes. His clothes said one thing about him but his gaze and his smile transmitted a completely different message. To me, he looked like a naughty boy who had been coached by his parents to behave properly during a solemn family event, but in his mind was counting down the minutes before he could throw away the suit and tie and go outside to climb a tree or run freely in the wild.

"Everyone in the club knew him and all liked him," his obituary said. I immediately felt the same too.

Later that day, I sat down and began reading the book properly. The inside of the back cover offered a brief description of William's poetry and why it merited publication. The anonymous note said of him:

> *Bell possessed a spontaneous eloquence combined with a strong sense of tradition. He used much conventional mythological imagery, but he made it his own, and to him it was the symbol of truth by which his personal feeling could best be expressed. His models were first Yeats and Pound and then beyond them early Italian and Provençal lyrics … many will come to look upon him not merely as a young man whose voice was prematurely silenced but as a poet whose imaginative work at its best was not unworthy of the early lyrics writers whom he studied.*

In the acknowledgment section, John Heath-Stubbs expressed his thanks to those among the family and friends who had assisted him in the preparation of the book. In particular, he mentioned Dr Harry C. Bell, William's father; Mr John Jones, a professor of English who also became Professor of Poetry at Oxford between 1978 and 1983; and Heathcote W. Garrod, a Fellow at Merton for over sixty years, Professor of Poetry at Oxford between 1923 and 1928 and a close friend of William's. Later in his life, he would become a Fellow of the British Academy. According to the historian Dacre Balsdon, it was Garrod who, during World War I, when accosted by a woman asking why he was not with the soldiers fighting to defend civilisation, replied, "Madam, I am the civilisation they are fighting to defend."

Although brief, Heath-Stubbs' introduction contained precious bits of information about William that would certainly help me to understand better his life and personality. The first one referred to the accident on the Matterhorn:

> *Together with Ian McKean, Bell had climbed the Matterhorn on the same day of the previous year, when they were accompanied by a guide. On this occasion, however, they decided, in order to save money, to dispense with guides.*

The fact that the three young lads had tried the ascent guideless was something that I was already aware of. Their reasons for doing it were less clear, though. The note published in *The Times* at the time of their death mentioned that they had run out of Swiss Francs. Now Heath-Stubbs seemed to confirm that report.

There was something terribly sad about the thought that they could have died because of their penniless state.

In this regard, one may be excused for thinking that Oxford or Cambridge universities at the end of the 1940s were the preserve of those born with a silver spoons in their mouths. However, William, Ian and James were not particularly wealthy – they were middle-class boys whose families enjoyed a relatively comfortable economic position. They could afford to travel to the Alps during their summer holidays, but it was obvious that money was very tight. Certainly none was available for fancy hotels or to buy champagne for a toast on reaching the summit – a custom among many better-off climbers, as John Tyndall describes in *Hours of Exercise in the Alps*: "the anxiety of the four hours before we reached the summit disappear like an unpleasant dream and with that perfect happiness which perfect health can alone impart, we consumed our cold mutton and champagne". For that reason, after reading Heath-Stubbs' introduction, the humble five pounds that William received from the Irvine Trust to help fund his climbing season in the Alps looked to me more valuable than ever.

The introductory chapter also described, although briefly, two other remarkable events in William's life. Apparently, in the summer of 1944 he had fallen from a considerable height while climbing in Snowdonia, and had to spend ten days in a hospital in Bangor recovering from his injuries. In relation to this accident, Heath-Stubbs mentioned that 'it seems strongly to have affected his imagination, and from this time onwards the image of falling from a height occurs in his poetry with an ominous frequency.'

The other outstanding episode took place in May 1946, when he received the Carnegie Medal for Bravery. This award is named after Andrew Carnegie, a Scotsman born in Dunfermline in 1835 who, at the age of thirteen, emigrated to America, eventually becoming one of the richest people in the country. A fervent philanthropist who by the time of his death in 1919 had given away about $350 million, Carnegie's wealth helped to establish numerous libraries, colleges, schools, non-profit organisations and associations all around the world. His is a sentence that I love: "The man who dies thus rich dies disgraced."

John Heath-Stubbs said that William had received the award in recognition for saving the life of a boy trapped on some cliffs near Arbroath, a mid-sized town on the coast of the North Sea, where, in 1320, the declaration of independence of Scotland was written by Chancellor of Scotland Bernard of Kilwinning and sent to Pope John XXII.

★

The following day I wrote an email to the Carnegie Hero Foundation requesting information about William's medal. I also called the local newspaper, *The Arbroath Herald*, in the hope that they could have something in their archives about the incident on the cliffs. If not, perhaps they could at least put me in contact with the local history society: one of those wonderful institutions in which amateur historians, in a completely altruistic way, help to keep alive the memory of hundreds of small towns and villages across Britain. As on many other occasions during my quest, Lady Fortune smiled on me, and the person who replied to my call at *The Herald*, Johnston Ralston, not only turned out to be a historian but also found my story quite exciting. He promised to take a look in the archives and, no more than an hour later, I received an email from him containing a detailed account of the events as they had been published by the Herald on Friday, 31 May 1946.

Arbroath Cliffs Tragedy

A cycle run undertaken by two Arbroath boys on Saturday ended in tragedy, one of them succumbing to injuries he received in a fall from the cliffs. The boys, Eric Macdonald (13) and James Napier (12), left the town in the early afternoon and made their way to Auchmithie and afterwards to Castlesea Bay, about a quarter of a mile from the village, on the side nearest Arbroath. After playing about there for a short time, they started to climb the cliffs, Napier leading. When Macdonald was about 40 feet up, he slipped, and fell to the rocks below. He received severe head injuries, and was rushed to Arbroath Infirmary where he died on Sunday afternoon without regaining consciousness.

Napier was unaware of his companion's mishap until he heard loose stones rattling and the thud as Macdonald struck the rocks. Fear froze him, and he remained stranded on a ledge 80 feet up. Sub-Lieutenant Robert Simmons, HMS Condor, and Stoker Lee, who were in the vicinity, heard

Napier's calls for help, and they found Macdonald lying unconscious at the bottom of the cliffs. While Lee was seeking assistance at Windyhills Farm, Sub-Lieut. Simmons made an effort to climb to Napier's assistance, but when about the same distance up as Macdonald he, too, slipped and fell to the rocks. In the meantime, Sub-Lieut. William, A. Bell, of HMS Condor, was lowered over the cliff by a rescue party and brought the boy Napier, who was little the worse for his experience, to the top. Sub-Lieut Simmons, who was conveyed to the Infirmary with the boy Macdonald, was found to be suffering from back injuries. His condition is improving.

The report from *The Herald* was so graphic that even from the comfort of my own house, I could visualise the terror of the Napier boy on those cliffs: the broken body of his friend Eric lying on the rocks, motionless. Help finally arrives and it seems like the nightmare will be over soon. However, the anguish spreads again among those present when the rock face below Sub-Lieutenant Robert Simmons gives way and he too crashes onto the beach, his piercing cry echoing in the ears of those watching powerless from the top of the cliff. Time is running out and nobody knows how long James will be able to hold on. Then William enters the scene – William, the Naval Reserve officer with the boyish smile; William, the poet; William, the climber; William, the hero-to-be.

I can imagine the screams of Eric Macdonald's mother when she arrives at the hospital only to find her baby boy dying. I can also picture the pats on William's back after he rescues James, the congratulations, the people who offer to buy him drinks. Yet his mind is completely absent, so concerned is he about the fate of his comrade Robert. William vaguely hears what people say to him, but it is the thud when Robert fell that resonates inside his head – the same sound that he heard when he fell in Wales two years earlier and his body crashed against the ground; the same sound that he recurrently still hears in his nightmares.

★

It is a few days later and the girl sitting next to me in Merton's reception area is getting her camera ready. However, she is not a tourist – her name is Julie and she is doing a PhD on book illustration in late medieval England. She is here to examine some of the incunabula preserved at the college library. For me, well, it's finally time to take a look to all the materials on William acquired by Merton – I have been looking forward to this moment since Julian Reid wrote to me while I was in Mauritius, more than a month ago.

The library is as beautiful and cosy as ever. It's a pity that I have to be back at the office in less than an hour because it would be great to relax and read, calmly, all the documents contained in the bulky folder that the librarian has put in front of me. But, alas, I have no time today. For that reason, rather than reading the documents, what I am doing is taking pictures of them: images that will be saved on my computer and that I will check later on the train on my way home, or over the weekend. For that reason, my attention is on getting the right focal length with my camera and the ISO sensitivity required to achieve a good resolution, rather than on the content of the letters and newspaper clippings that I have in front of me.

However, amid the pile of documents that I am photographing, there are two in particular that catch my attention. The first one is a black and white postcard sent by William from Zermatt in 1947, when he first climbed the Matterhorn. The pyramidal shape of the mountain entirely dominates the picture. Below, the entrance of the Zmutt valley is visible as well, as is a good portion of the Edelweissweg – the steep hill just above Zermatt, from where the panorama is breath-taking; on a clear day you can enjoy a sweeping view of the north face of the Matterhorn as well as the Hörnli and Zmutt ridges, with the Breithorn, Lyskamm and Monte Rosa glowing to your left.

In the postcard, Zermatt is barely developed – nothing like the hive of activity the town currently is. On the left bank of the river Vispa only a few houses are visible here and there. In fact, the city has changed so much that is difficult for me to find any reference, with the exception of two iconic buildings. One is the Great Hotel Zermatterhoff, built in 1879, which together with the Hotel Monte Rosa is a symbol of the status of Zermatt as a prime climbing and mountaineering destination since the second half of nineteenth century. The other one is Saint Peter's church, beside which is situated the Mountaineers' Cemetery, and where unknown to him at the time he sent the postcard, William would be buried the following summer.

The other document that I paused to read was a letter written by William's father, Dr Harry C. Bell, on 2 August 1948 – a week after the accident on the Matterhorn. The letter was addressed to Ian Davie, one of William's best friends, and clearly it was a response to a previous condolence note sent by Ian. The letter, although brief, is a dignified and emotive testament to William's parents' affection for him. A sentence in particular caught my attention: "Perhaps we loved him too much, but it would have been impossible to love him less."

Sometimes only twelve, fifteen words are all that are required to tell a long story or to express the deepest feeling. Like the sentence on their tombstone – 'friends from Oxford killed together on the Matterhorn' – that so intensely moved me that day back in Zermatt, what Dr Bell wrote a week after the death of this elder son accompanied me for the rest of the day, and for many more days to come.

12. The first snow of the season

I had a farm in Africa, at the foot of the Ngong Hill.
Karen Blixen

Buying a present is never an easy task. Obviously, I am not talking about buying any present – everybody can do that. What I am talking about is finding that rare something that will exactly embody your feelings towards the recipient; this is much harder to accomplish. The situation only becomes worse if you don't personally know that person, as was the case with me and Donald McKean and David Ogilvie. For that reason, one week before flying to Edinburgh to meet them, my big dilemma was what on Earth I could take them, as the last thing that I wanted was to arrive at their homes empty-handed.

A good bottle of red wine is usually a safe solution, albeit an unimaginative one. However, I ruled it out mostly because I didn't know whether, being in their late eighties, they would appreciate alcohol. Fine biscuits or chocolates also come in handy on an occasion like this, but they were ruled out as well following a similar principle.

So, what could I get them? The solution came early on a Monday morning, while I was at the office. Although still October, temperatures had dropped substantially during the weekend to a point where they were barely above zero. One of my colleagues came in from the street, shivering from the cold and yelling "I need a warm cup of tea!" At once I knew that this was the answer I had been looking for! Everybody drinks tea in Britain; everybody loves tea. It was a perfect and simple idea.

However, it couldn't be *any* tea – certainly not the kind of tea that can be bought in a supermarket or a corner shop. No, it had to be the best tea that I could find. That was the second part of the puzzle, because although everybody may drink tea in Britain, I do not. In fact, I really dislike it, which means that I have no idea why one tea is better than another. A tea connoisseur was needed, but alas, all that was available to me that morning was the Internet. In case you have never tried, if you type 'best tea' into Google, believe me, you will get something like a hundred responses from all kind of retailers and shops, all of them claiming to sell the best tea under the sun. Under these circumstances, it was impossible to make an informed decision.

Then inspiration struck me. A few days earlier I had been reading about the preparations for the 1922 British expedition to Mount Everest and how Fortnum and Mason, the quintessential delicatessen store in London, had supplied them with sixty tins of quail in foie gras and four dozen bottles of champagne, appropriately named *Montebello*. Founded in 1707, it is one of my favourite shops in London and whenever I am around I like to pop in, even if most of the time I don't buy anything. For sure, Fortnum and Mason was the perfect place to find the perfect tea.

After visiting their website, I bought four different blends of tea – two for the McKeans and two for the Ogilvies – all of them contained in charmingly decorated caddies. There was a small problem, though; as I ordered the tea on Tuesday evening, it was not guaranteed that it could be delivered to my house by Friday lunch time, when Marian and I were due to leave for the airport for our early evening flight to the capital of Scotland. The response from Fortnum and Mason's customer service was exceptional – after I explained who the tea was for and how much this visit meant to me, they agreed to make an exception to their own rules and send the parcel directly to Edinburgh so it would be already waiting for me there. In this way we could go to the offices of the delivery company as early as possible on Saturday morning, and collect it personally.

It worked. On Saturday, at 7am, Marian and I were in the back seat of a cab on our way to the depot, which was somewhere between the airport and Murrayfield, the iconic home of the Scottish rugby. In compensation for the early wake-up, not only I did get my precious tea, but we were also rewarded with a crisp, beautiful autumn dawn, the gentle light of the morning illuminating the monument to Scott in Princess Street with delicate shades of ochre. The stillness of the morning was barely broken by some noisy drunks here and there, returning home after a long night of fun. The start of the day was excellent and the weather forecast for the rest of the day was promising as well – although the temperatures were not expected to be very high, there would be clear skies all across Scotland and plenty of sunshine.

★

David Ogilvie and his wife, Hillary, live in Bloomfield, a small hamlet in the very heart of the Scottish Borders, about 70 miles south of Edinburgh. Our plan was to get a bus to the nearby village of Saint Boswells, where David would be waiting for us. From there he would drive us to his house, about five minutes away. David had kindly invited us to have lunch with them, so we left Edinburgh at around ten in the morning in order to be in Bloomfield no more than a couple of hours later.

The trip to Saint Boswells was delightful. Once we left Edinburgh behind, the rolling hills of the Borders appeared splendidly in front of us, the lush meadows alive with flocks of peaceful sheep, the banks of the numerous streams along the way full of trees already alight with the colours of the autumn. One place in particular caught my imagination: Dun Law hill and its wind farm. The silhouette of the turbines against the horizon reminded me of modern giants perpetually waiting for a Don Quixote to engage them in fierce combat. To make the place even more exciting, the whole area was covered in snow. When we had arrived in Edinburgh the previous night it was quite cold, the thermometers in the streets marking minus one or two degrees. However, the sky had been so clear that it was difficult to believe that it had been snowing just a few miles to the south. It was the first snow of the season, David told us later, and also the first time in more than forty years that it had snowed in the Borders in October. The snow was melting pretty fast in the sunshine but it made the journey more extraordinary than it already was.

Had this been a normal journey I'd certainly have enjoyed it more. However, there was nothing normal about it. It was so extraordinary that, from time to time, I had to figuratively pinch myself to be sure that I was really there: in Scotland, on my way to visit James Ogilvie's brother. In addition, the following day I would meet Donald McKean. 'Surreal' was the word that Marian and I used most often that weekend when we tried to explain what we were living through. Being on a bus, in the middle of a remote place, visiting someone you have never met before in your life and whose name meant absolutely nothing to you barely four months ago, to talk about a relative who died more than half a century ago – this is the kind of stuff you see in movies, not something that happens in real life, to ordinary people like us. Yes, definitely, it was surreal. Maybe for that reason, during the whole trip from Edinburgh, I felt like a million of butterflies were nesting in my stomach.

When we arrived at Saint Boswells, David Ogilvie was already waiting for us. I didn't have a picture of him but he was the only person at the bus stop so it necessarily had to be him. Still, I hesitated for a fraction of a second as the man standing there did not by any means look like a man in his mid-eighties. "Seventy or 72, tops," I thought. He was wearing a green olive cotton sweater and blue trousers. He was tanned, and projected vitality and energy. When he saw us descending from the bus, he just smiled and said, "I am David, welcome." His handshake was firm and I immediately liked him.

On the way to his house, down a single-track road surrounded by beautiful fields, he told us about the recent trip that he and Hillary had taken to Bilbao, in Spain, and how they had enormously enjoyed the exhibits at the Guggenheim Museum. They also went to the south of France and while there Hillary fell sick. Fortunately, she was totally recovered now. David spoke highly of the attention they received in the French hospital: the quality of the doctors, the individual room they enjoyed and even how the nurses brought Hillary Chanel No5 every morning. Although it was a very good ice-breaking conversation, I was still quite nervous. So, when the opportunity came I delivered the little speech that I had carefully prepared during the bus journey. I wanted to let David know how grateful we were for his kind invitation. Even more importantly, I wanted to reassure him that our intention was not to cause any distress. In fact, I told him, we would totally understand if there was something that they preferred not to talk about. He just paused for a second, before saying "Don't worry, all this is way back in the past so there is no pain anymore – it's emotional but not distressing." For us, it was an immense relief to hear David say that.

Bloomfield is on top of a small hill, protected from the north wind by dense lines of trees. It is not even a village – there are barely three or four houses, and a couple of large farm buildings along the road. In front of The Ogilvies' cottage was a beautiful, gleaming red phone box, which David proudly told us that they helped to maintain. When we arrived, Hillary was waiting for us outside the house with a welcoming smile. She was dressed in a casual way, as if she had been pruning her roses in the garden barely five minutes ago. It was evident that she had been a very attractive woman in her youth. Indeed, she was still very beautiful, with sparkling eyes and graceful, charming manners. During our short trip from the bus stop David had helped us to be progressively more at ease, but it was Hillary who made us feel completely at home. From the first moment, she treated us as if we were a couple of old friends visiting after spending a time abroad.

The cottage was homely and cosy, with plenty of family pictures and some framed drawings done by their grandchildren. In the living room a blazing fire in the fireplace created a warm, comfortable atmosphere. The opposite wall was occupied by a bookshelf packed with beautiful, old books. Scattered around the room there were two or three music stands and some instruments, including a violin. "We like to play them with our grandchildren, when they come to visit us," Hillary explained. The kitchen was spacious and full of light, with one window opening onto the back garden and the other one to the front. On both sides of the house there were several bird feeders filled with peanuts. During the time we were there, much to Marian's delight (she loves birds) the flow of blue tits, sparrows, and robins was incessant.

During lunch, much of the conversation revolved around one of their sons, James, who not only shared a name with his uncle but also his passion for mountains. With unconcealed pride, they told us that he was half way to completing the Seven Summits – also called the 'Grand Slam' of mountaineering. James had already climbed Mount Everest in Asia, Kilimanjaro in Africa, Mount McKinley in North America and Aconcagua in South America. At that moment, he was raising funds for an expedition to Mount Vinson in Antarctica, which he planned to carry out in 2015. We also talked about their life in Africa, during the 1950s. For a few years they had lived in Zanzibar, but also in Zambia, where Hillary carried out topographic surveys. Armed with just a few aerial photographs, and driving her own Land Rover, she had to spend weeks in the bush to complete the work, which often took her to the most remote areas of the country. Most of the time she was completely by herself.

Because of my job I have also travelled extensively in places such as Nigeria, Kenya, and Mozambique. I have visited many other sub-Saharan countries too. Still, what Hillary described to us that day was something that seemed to belong to a long-gone era. It was rather like having lunch with Karen Blixen – the author of *Out of Africa*, and once described as 'the best writer and the worst farmer that ever lived in Africa' – as she recounted to us the flight of the eagles in the Ngong Hills. At that moment, I recalled a paragraph from Karen's book that I have always loved:

> *'If I know a song of Africa, of the giraffe and the African new moon lying on her back, of the ploughs in the fields and the sweaty faces of the coffee pickers, does Africa know a song of me? Will the air over the plain quiver with a colour that I have had on, or the children invent a game in which my name is, or the full moon throw a shadow over the gravel of the drive that was like me?'*

After lunch we sat in front of the fire to enjoy a cup of coffee, the whole room filled with the evocative scent of wood smoke. It was only then that we talked for the first time about James – David's older brother – and his two companions, William and Ian. It was also then they told us that on Wednesday they had visited Donald and Marianne McKean at their house in Edinburgh.

A couple of weeks earlier, Donald had asked me whether I could give him David's telephone number. "I would like to talk to him," was all he had said. I happily obliged without knowing that the families had lost all contact at some point after the accident. As a matter of fact, they hadn't had any news of each other for more than sixty years.

David and Hillary seemed to have fond memories of their meeting with the McKeans. Apparently, they had lived in the same neighbourhood in Edinburgh for more than three decades without being aware of it. David told us that Donald was in a delicate state of health, with his eyesight deteriorating quite fast. "But his memory is simply astonishing. He remembers everything that happened in the summer of 1948."

The two couples had spent the afternoon chatting, sharing memories, and talking about their lives, their children and grandchildren. Naturally, they also talked about me. I presume that each of them wanted to know what the other family thought about my project and my intentions. David told me that Donald McKean was as keen as he was to provide as much support as possible. However, he added that Donald was also concerned about getting all the facts correct in my book. "That's why I came to Scotland," was my response. "That is why I wanted to talk to you and Donald – because I want to be as accurate as possible."

Hearing about the reunion of the two families, after so much time had gone by, was heart-warming. Since the moment back in Mauritius when I learned about the existence of David Ogilvie and Donald McKean, I had feared that by unearthing the story of their brothers I could bring anguish to their lives. To know that because of my quest the Ogilvies and McKeans had met again, and that they had really enjoyed the encounter, with all that it meant, was a fantastic feeling. It was a huge relief too. On our way back to Edinburgh I recall telling Marian that even if this book was never finished, the fact that I had contributed to making that reunion happen meant that all my efforts would have been absolutely worthwhile.

During our conversation, I showed David and Hillary all the documents I had managed to gather up to that moment: the picture of the tombstone in Zermatt, the scans of the registers in Balliol and Merton, copies of the obituaries in the journal of the Oxford University Mountaineering Club and pictures of

130

William's documents recently acquired by Merton's library. Most of the material was completely new to David and Hillary, and they examined it with careful attention. They also asked many questions. At some point, I also showed them a picture of the Matterhorn that I had taken the previous summer. Taken from Zermatt, the mountain glittered in all its majesty in the late light of the afternoon. David looked at it for a long time and finally said, "You know, sometimes it amazes me that James loved mountains so much because the truth is that he was neither very tall nor very strong physically. Or at least, that's the way I remember him."

When I asked him about his brother's character, his response was surprising, "James could be very annoying sometimes: he always wanted to be first in everything and was extremely competitive." However, there was not a hint of reproach or criticism in his words. On the contrary, he was just describing something common in the relations between most brothers – the rivalry between them, which often the younger one, being smaller and usually weaker, finds overwhelming. In a way it was quite nice that David had said that, because it meant that James was not a fading memory of the past or someone put on a pedestal and idealised in death. David talked about his older brother as if he was there with us at that very moment, having a cup of coffee in front of the chimney, and he said to him, half jokingly, "Oh, James, you were such a pain when we were children."

We also talked a lot about James's principles and ethics. I raised this issue because after reading Heath-Stubbs' introduction to *Mountains Beneath the Horizon*, it was evident that William was very conservative, at least politically speaking. Ian, on the contrary, was the chairman of the Labour Party at Oxford University, a quite strong political stance at that time. Separated by ideology and yet brought together by their love for mountains, it was easy to picture the two climbing partners having ardent discussions on politics in the hut, in the aftermath of a climbing day. In this scenario, I wondered what James, the third in the party, would have said or thought. "James had a very strong social conscience. He was very generous and always cared about those who were less fortunate than him. So, in this respect, my guess is that he was closer to Ian's ideas than to those of William," David Ogilvie said. "If anything," he added, "the war underpinned James's vision of what was fair and what wasn't from a social perspective."

David told us that during the war James had served as a trooper, the lowest rank in the Royal Scot Greys, living and fighting side by side every day with soldiers from the most underprivileged backgrounds in Scotland: people who, in most cases, had endured a much tougher upbringing than his; people without any expectations for the future beyond working in a factory or returning to the farm once the war was over; people for whom Oxford University was as remote a place as Mars. Wars, however, tend to create extremely resilient bonds between those who fight in them. In the words of Glenn Gray in *The Warriors: Reflections on Men in Battle,* 'Danger breaks down the barriers of the self and gives soldiers a higher sense of community.' That happened to James, David told us, to the point where he even rejected a commission to become an officer. Instead, he remained a trooper, so that he could end the war with those men with whom he had started it. Only when he was serving in India with the 8th Light Cavalry Regiment, one of the oldest (it was created in 1787) and most distinguished regiments in the history of the British military presence in India, did he accept a commission as a Second Lieutenant.

The most emotional part of the conversation occurred when Hillary told us how she heard about the accident. Her family and the Ogilvies were quite close in 1948 and although she was barely a teenager, she still remembered quite well how they heard the news. "They had disappeared for two days, and in the afternoon my father came to tell us that they had been found. For a fraction of a second I thought he meant that they were alive, and my reaction was 'That's wonderful', but then my father said that all of them were dead. It was devastating." She also recalled how her mother muttered something like, 'What a waste of life…', at which point, Hillary's father said something that she had never forgotten, despite all the time that had gone by since, "It is not a waste of life: if young people didn't dare to take risks then the world would be a much worse place."

"They belonged," Hillary continued, "to a generation of Britons who lived through the most extraordinary circumstances. A generation forced to make enormous sacrifices in the face of the most adverse conditions. It was a generation for whom words like 'patriotism' or 'generosity' really meant something. They were not just words for them. And it was a generation with high ideals and aspirations too. We owe them a lot – Britain is what it is today because of them and for that reason not only do they deserve to be remembered but also celebrated."

In a soft tone of voice, David also told us about the devastating effect that the death of James had on the whole family. "It was a tough time for everybody but I guess that it was particularly hard for my father, who would die less than a year later." Sir Frederick, 'Freddie', Wolff Ogilvie, James and David's father, had been a Second Lieutenant with the Bedfordshire Regiment during World War I. As such, he had taken part in the many combat operations over the notorious Hill 60, in the battle of Ypres, in 1915. It was there that he lost his left arm. That was a powerful reminder of the indissoluble duties that came with the privilege of being British in the first part of the twentieth century – two generations of Britons, fathers and sons, united by the sacrifices they made on the battlefields of the two world wars.

David also talked about his mother, Mary Ogilvie, 'An extraordinary woman', who after the sudden death of her husband and son in such a short period of time, became the cornerstone of support for the whole family. In 1953 she became the Principal of St Anne's College in Oxford: a role in which she served for thirteen years, until 1966. That was not just a period of growth and expansion at the College, with new buildings and more students, but also one of academic excellence. At the end of her principalship St Anne's came top of the Norrington Table, which ranks the results of the colleges of the University of Oxford. I was so intrigued by David's mother and the fortitude she showed in bringing up her family, that after returning from Scotland I went to St Anne's, where there is still a portrait of her. It shows an elderly lady with her white hair in an old-fashioned bun, and the most delightful, playful smile on her face. Considering the innovations that she introduced at St Anne's, such as Oxford's first ever nursery for the children of staff, and transforming the College into the first ever mixed graduate institute (the idea of boys and girls living and studying together had certainly been quite a revolution back in the 1950s), it was clear that she was someone well ahead of her time.

It was almost six o'clock by the time we had to leave. While we were getting ready to go, David excused himself and went upstairs. After a couple of minutes he returned with some papers. One of the documents was an unbound booklet with a dark-brown paper cover, forty or fifty pages long, clearly yellowing from the passing of time. "It's for you," he said. The title was *Letters of James William Ogilvie*. I looked at him, unable to conceal my surprise. "It was my father's wish that we put together all his correspondence." I took a quick look at it – most of the letters seemed to have been written during World War II but there were also letters that James sent to his family while serving in India. At the beginning there were also a couple of missives from Rugby School, where he studied. "The other document," David continued, "is a letter that James wrote in April 1948 to our uncle Robert, who lived in Kuala Lumpur at that time. It is a very detailed description of the trip that he made with William and Ian to the central Scottish Highlands, during the Easter vacation, as a kind of a preparation for the summer climbing season in the Alps. As you can see, James loved writing long letters," he added with a smile.

At first I was hesitant to accept them – it felt somehow inappropriate for me to take with me such valuable family documents, particularly the booklet, which was clearly an original version printed in the 1950s. Noticing my doubts, David said, "Don't worry, I still have a couple more copies." And as if he thought that it was not enough to convince me, he reassuringly added, "I cannot think of a better use for them."

Before leaving, I asked David and Hillary two favours. The first was whether I could take a picture of them. They gladly posed for me: Hillary with her beautiful, natural smile; David with a direct, frank glance. I have their picture in front of me while I am writing this and it is one of my most precious treasures of the entire quest. The second favour was that he write something, whatever he wanted, in William's book. That night, back in the hotel, I read it for the first time. He had written: "In memory of three friends."

As we were saying our good-byes to Hillary she noticed Marian's scarf and mentioned a couple of times how beautiful it was. That night we agreed that as soon as we returned to Oxford we would visit the shop where Marian had bought it, and buy the same one for her. The Ogilvies had been so kind and generous to us that it was the least that we could do.

13. The picture

*The highlight of my childhood was making my brother laugh
so hard that food came out his nose.*
Garrison Keillor

In contrast with the clear skies of the previous day, Sunday dawned grey and rainy in Edinburgh. Our meeting with Donald McKean was scheduled for 2pm at his home, which in theory left us plenty of time in the morning to do whatever we wanted. However, we were not in the right mind-set for sightseeing or shopping; with so many amazing things happening, I guess that we just wanted time to savour them without unnecessary distractions. For that reason I thought it was an excellent idea when Marian proposed that we go to a warm, quiet coffee shop and spend the morning reading, or in my case, reviewing the notes that I had taken the previous day during our meeting with the Ogilvies.

When it comes to beautiful coffee places in Edinburgh, the obvious choice is The Elephant House, with its rooms overlooking the castle and the Greyfriars Cemetery. The graveyard is quite well known because of two very different characters associated with it. One of them is Greyfriars Bobby, the little terrier who in the nineteenth century supposedly spent fourteen years guarding the grave of his owner. Bobby's limitless loyalty moved the hearts of the citizens of the city who, in turn, erected a statue at the main entrance of the cemetery in his honour. Nowadays, no tourist worth their salt goes to Edinburgh without taking a picture of what is probably the most famous dog in Scotland.

The other notorious Greyfriars guest, though, is far darker. In 1679, the southern section of the graveyard was used as a prison for over one thousand supporters of the National Covenant who had been defeated during the Scottish Civil War. For over four months, the Covenanters were held prisoners there without any shelter, being fed less than 3 ounces of bread a day. Most of them died. Today, the area of the graveyard known as the Covenanter's Prison is the realm of the Mackenzie poltergeist, one of the best-documented cases of paranormal activity in the world, with at least 350 reported attacks (including unexplained bites and scratches) and 170 reports of people collapsing in Greyfriars since 1998. I visited the place in 2005 and I have to confess that I have never been so scared in my entire life.

The Elephant House is quite famous too, as it was there that J.K.Rowling wrote some of her early *Harry Potter* books. A theory shared by many 'Potterologists' is that Hogwarts, the school of witchcraft and wizardry attended by Harry, may be based on the imposing George Heriot's School, perfectly visible at the other side of the cemetery. The Elephant House has also provided inspiration to other authors, including Ian Rankin, author of the bestselling novels of Detective Inspector John Rebus, and to Alexander McCall-Smith, the author of the series of *The No.1 Ladies' Detective Agency*. "Maybe it is the water that they serve in this café, or something else, but I definitely could use some inspiration today," I recall telling Marian. However, it was not meant to be, because the place was full of Japanese tourists and not a single table was available. As a result, we spent the morning in a cosy though less prominent coffee place near the university, reading and, from time to time, raising our heads to vacantly watch raindrops against the windows.

Around 1pm we walked towards the McKeans' home, which is on the south side of the city, in a nice residential area with dense trees and manicured lawns. When we arrived, Marianne was outside in the front garden; we barely had to say anything, as she immediately recognised us and with a lovely smile invited us to come in.

Admittedly, I was more worried about meeting Donald than David. For David Ogilvie, the loss of his brother was indeed a terrible family tragedy, but a tragedy in which he had no part whatsoever. By contrast, Donald McKean was on the Matterhorn that dreadful day, back in 1948. He slept in the Hörnli hut with William, Ian and James, and most likely he was the last person they talked to in the morning, before starting the ascent. After the accident, it was Donald, as the closest relative of one of the deceased, who surely had to deal with the authorities, as well as all the paperwork and bureaucracy. Perhaps he even had to identify the bodies once they were recovered. It was he who would have had to respond to the endless questions from the families, when he called back home to let them know that they had all died. It was likely that Donald asked himself 'what if' countless times in the next few days or weeks, 'What if I hadn't felt sick that night?' 'What if I had been on the ridge with them, could I have somehow contributed to prevent the accident?' I wouldn't be surprised at all if he even felt an element of guilt for being alive – the 'survivor guilt'. And all this happened when he was just nineteen years old – a teenager, almost a boy. Yes, I got the nervous feeling that today's meeting was going to be more tense and difficult.

Thankfully, all my concerns disappeared as soon as I met him. Donald is the kind of person who radiates kindness: someone who can be comprehensively described using just three words – a good man. Regrettably, his health was not good and, as David had mentioned, his vision had significantly deteriorated. Despite being more or less the same age, the McKeans looked much more fragile than Hillary and David Ogilvie. However, first impressions can sometimes be deceptive, and during our time there I was impressed by the agility that both Donald and Marianne displayed. At one point I recall Donald performing an incredible balancing act on his chair, leaning right back to reach a spoon from the drawer behind him in a way that certainly belied his years, and whilst they may have had some physical problems, by no means were Donald and

Marianne disabled people. Indeed, their tenacity in old age was nothing short of inspirational.

Donald's predominant physical feature is his height – he is indeed very tall – as well as his slim build. However, the thing I remember the most about him is his voice: a melodious, comforting voice, like that of a radio broadcaster. That he had such a nice voice was not entirely surprising, as he had enjoyed a long professional career in the academic world – more precisely at the University of Edinburgh, where he had been a professor in the School of Chemistry.

After some small-talk, our attention turned to their summer trip in 1948. Using his own diary as well as his brother's as a reference, Donald had prepared a brief outline of the weeks they spent in the Alps, including the places they had visited and the peaks they had climbed. These notes were priceless to me, as I was still completely in the dark regarding the whereabouts of the OUMC group before their attempt on the Matterhorn. Among the documentation acquired by Merton, there was a letter sent by William to his friend Ian Davie the previous summer, where he explained that after spending some time rock-climbing in Arolla, they had gone to Zermatt via the Haute Route – the same route that Marian and I had trekked in August 2012. For that reason, my first question to Donald was whether they had done something similar a year later, in 1948.

"No, we didn't," he explained. "In 1948 we started in Martigny, in Switzerland, and spent about a good week, I think, at the hut on the Trient Plateau, doing a lot of climbing. Then we crossed into France, had a night in the Argentière hut, on the north-east side of the Mont Blanc massif, from where we climbed the Tour Noir. After descending to Chamonix, we took the train to Montenvers and walked up the Mer de Glace to the Requin hut. There we stayed for three nights. On the second day we went up to do a small peak called Aiguille du Plan. After that we went up to the Col du Geant and stayed a night in the Torino hut.

"The following day, we took the cableway to descend to Courmayeur, on the Italian side of Mont Blanc. We had a great ice-cream there," said Donald to a chorus of laughs. From Courmayeur, the OUMC group – which included not only William Bell, the McKean brothers and James Ogilvie, but also Ted Simpson and Jim Holt – returned to Switzerland via Col Ferret.

To my surprise, I was quite familiar with most of the places mentioned by Donald. Some of them, like the Swiss village of Trient, or Courmayeur in Italy, are part of the Tour of Mont Blanc – a circular 105-mile trek around the Mont Blanc massif with a combined height gain and loss of around 33,000 feet. Marian and I had completed this route clockwise in 2010, and again a year later, anti-clockwise. The Tour of Mont Blanc, or TMB, is one of the most traditional mountain treks in Europe. In fact, the first recorded TMB took place in 1767 when Horace Bénédict de Saussure set out from Chamonix with friends on an exploration trip that included the Bonhomme Col and the Seigne Col in France, Courmayeur in Italy, and the Grand Saint Bernard Pass in Switzerland before returning to Chamonix. The TMB is not as hard and demanding as the Haute Route, and perhaps for that reason is more popular. Also, because of its circular nature, the trekkers on the TMB enjoy wonderful views of the Mont Blanc massif almost every single day, from every direction. So impressive are the views that Marian and I would spend some time at the end of every day, with a pair of binoculars and a map, trying to identify every peak and col in the massif. Hence my familiarity with most of the mountains climbed by the OUMC group in 1948.

According to Donald, the Mont Blanc massif was always their primary destination. In fact, they spent almost three weeks there and, contrary to my initial guess, climbing the Matterhorn was never part of their plan. In fact, going to Zermatt was a last-minute decision.

"Once we arrived in Zermatt, we stayed in the Schönbiel hut as it was the most economic accommodation available," Donald continued. "We attempted several climbs in the area. The Weisshorn was one of them, but basically there was too much snow and we had to abandon it – we found ourselves early in the morning in an area with a lot of avalanche debris, which is not a healthy place to be. Also the weather conditions were bad. The following day I had to stay in Zermatt, as I was not feeling very well, but the others successfully climbed the Monte Rosa, which was quite an undertaking. They were sufficiently strong and determined and when they came back they decided to have a go at the Matterhorn."

"My brother had climbed the mountain a year earlier, in 1947. The weather was good that year. William Bell had also been up there that summer, although I don't know the details. So, out of the three, James Ogilvie was the only one who had not yet climbed the Matterhorn. So the idea was, 'Here we are in Zermatt, the Hörnli ridge is easy and we will do it before we go.' There was an element of lack of awareness regarding the precise conditions on this very easy route. So, from a mountaineering point of view, the mistake, if you want to call it that way, was lack of perception," Donald concluded with a note of sorrow in his voice.

Donald also climbed the Matterhorn many, many years later, in 1980, at the end of a family holiday in Zermatt. He was 52 at the time. On that occasion, he hired the services of a local guide. "After spending four weeks in the Alps I was pretty fit. Still, all my attention was entirely on keeping up with the guide. The climb went quite well. That day there was only one other party on the mountain, which is quite unusual. After we reached the top, the guide wanted to smoke but he inadvertently dropped the box of cigarettes on the snow slope that runs continuously to the north face and then drops for 3,000 feet. He didn't want to lose his cigarettes, so he unroped and started getting down to get them. I recall that I said to myself 'If he goes down over the edge, I am here, unroped, and stuck on my own, how I am going to descend?' Luckily he came back, we roped up and safely went down."

Now, Donald's voice was becoming increasingly agitated. "By climbing the Matterhorn in 1980 I was able to understand that even during this easy ascent, there was this serious risk of a stone-fall, which I am pretty certain was the cause of the 1948 accident. But nobody knows. Apparently there was a report stating that the accident was watched by someone with a big telescope. This report, which was never shown to me, said that this person saw the climbers falling. Whether they were on the way up or on their way down, is uncertain but I would have thought that they were still on their way up." He went silent for a second and then, deliberately, he said, "For some time after the accident I had nightmares of being back on the mountain – unpleasant and grotesque nightmares."

The conversation seemed to be drifting towards some dangerous, slippery terrain – that of bad memories and raw feelings barely buried by the passing of time. It was evident that for Donald McKean the loss of his brother was not entirely a matter of the past. So I interrupted him as tactfully as possible – I didn't want him, however generously, to keep talking about something so evidently painful as the accident just because he thought that was where my main interest lay. I therefore repeated what I had told David Ogilvie the previous day – my priority was not finding out how William, Ian and James had died; instead I wanted to focus on how they lived amid the extraordinary circumstances that surrounded then. "For me," I said, "it is much more important to know how Ian's political commitment was forged than about the accident." Donald nodded; Marianne, his wife, looked kindly at me, with what seemed to be a smile of relief.

By then we had already moved to a cosy living room, with a beautiful view of the back garden. "Well," he continued, "your interest in his ideas and vision of life brings me very naturally onto describing the material I have here. My brother wrote a diary starting from, I think, his second year of school, in 1940 or 1941 at Tonbridge, 'till 1948."

Again, moving in a nimble manner, he reached for a small pile of little notebooks behind him. They were Ian's diaries that he had mentioned in his first communication with me. "In the last weeks, since you first called me, I have gone through them all again, with difficulty," he added laughing. "Somehow very bad handwriting."

"My daughter and one of her daughters have been scanning all this so you can have it," Marianne added. "Sometimes children can be very useful," Donald remarked, and we all laughed.

Clearly the mood had changed and we were no longer on the Hörnli ridge, under the sombre shadow of the Matterhorn, that morning in 1948. We were in a completely different place now, definitely a brighter and more agreeable one: a place where Ian was not about to die; a place where Donald could talk about his brother with pride and true admiration. Yes, admiration was, Marian and I agreed once we had left, the word that better described what Donald still felt for his brother, all these years after his death. If a certain level of sibling rivalry seemed to be present in the relationship between James and David Ogilvie, in the case of the McKeans it was evident that Donald had idolised his older brother: everything he did and said that afternoon denoted it. For us it was a rare privilege to be witness to such an intimate expression of love and affection.

A key factor in the closeness between Donald and Ian McKean was the fact that they really did a lot of things together, such as attending Oxford at the same time, despite the fact that Donald was three years younger. Unlike William Bell, who had spent two years reading Physics before joining the Royal Naval Volunteer Reserve, Ian McKean went to Oxford only once the war was over, after serving in the Intelligence Corps at Bletchley Park. By that time, Donald had also finished school, so they went to university together.

"One of the first things that I was told was going to be very exciting was a meeting of the Socialist Club. Apparently, there was going to be a tremendous row and a split that would lead to the formation of a new Labour Club, which was firmly oriented towards democratic socialism as opposed to the Communist Marxists. I was not into politics in any way myself, but I still attended and I remember the passionate speeches, and the people saying 'Comrades, this; comrades that.' My brother made an important contribution to the constitution of the new Labour Club, and one of my daughters, while scanning the diaries, noticed that there were a lot of references to that in them."

At this point, I asked Donald McKean the same question that I had asked David Ogilvie the day before: how it was possible that boys that came from such comfortable backgrounds had such progressive political ideas.

"My mother was an English Presbyterian," Donald explained, "and when we lived near London, we attended a Congregational church. My brother became a member of the church, which is something that he took very seriously. The Congregationalists had, at that time, very radical political views, very far from the position of the Tories. So I guess that the progressive political ideas of my brother had a lot to do with his Christian roots."

"In line with the Scandinavian social democracy of the post-war period," Marianne added. "Have you seen the letter from James Ogilvie to his uncle? It is very funny as he makes a comment about

145

going to climb with William, who is a high Tory and an Anglican, and with Ian, who is a Congregationalist and a Socialist."

"Sometimes there were tremendous discussions in the huts," Donald said, "between William Bell and my brother, although always in good spirit. My brother was a skilful arguer while William was not that kind of thinker at all, but an emotional, poetic kind of person. I remember one occasion when my brother told William that he was not arguing straight, and he didn't take it kindly," Donald said to more laughs from us. "Ian was a brilliant debater, which was one of the things that came out from all his interactions with the Labour Club. He received many invitations to speak at different Labour constituencies. With his preparation and speaking skills it was very likely that he would have been red-carpeted to become an MP wherever he wanted. He was highly regarded in the party and this consideration is reflected in the hand-written letter that Clement Attlee, the prime minister, sent to my parents after the accident."

We talked about many other things that afternoon. For example, their family experience during the war. "When we were moved to Rustington, my accountant uncle was already living there and he became the 'Captain Mainwaring' of the local Home Guard, while my Scottish engineer father became the sergeant. My mother claimed that *Dad's Army* was very true to life!" Donald told us with a gleaming smile on his face, remembering what seemed to be hard but happy family times. However, his expression changed completely when he started talking again about what had happened after the accident.

He explained that as the first reports appeared in the press there were many rumours and inventions about how the accident had taken place. One journalist even wrote that Donald had been part of the climbing party that morning, which was completely untrue. At some point in the following few days, he had confronted the journalist to ask him to rectify the story. "That's why I am so sensitive about getting all the facts right."

We also talked at length about Ian's character. According to Donald, he was a voracious reader and possessed an enormous collection of books. Extremely brilliant from an intellectual point of view, he also excelled at different sports; he was a very good rugby player and a decent rower, "although I was a better rock-climber than him," Donald told us with a proud smile. The combination of academic excellence and sporting achievements made Ian quite popular at his school, Rugby. "Yet, he was quite modest; there was always a natural modesty about him. The thing that I remember most about my brother is that he never made anybody feel belittled – in fact he reprimanded me a couple of times for being boastful. He was also kind to everybody, and he had this rare ability of being able to know exactly what to say and how to behave with all kinds of people in all kinds of circumstances."

The more we talked, the more I understood why Donald admired his brother Ian so much. He had been a reference point, a role model for him. He was also a protector. "In Rugby, being three years my senior, he always looked after me," said Donald. It was also Ian who introduced Donald to hill-walking, "He took me hill-walking when I was thirteen or fourteen because he was afraid I was not doing enough exercise. I loved it because it was a good introduction to female company," he added with a naughty smile. After some laughs, we talked about their excursions to the Lake District and also to Skye, where Ian taught Donald the basics of rock-climbing.

I was amazed to find out that in 1949, a year after his brother's death, Donald had been climbing on the French side of the Pyrenees with a group of friends. At one point, they inadvertently crossed the border to Spain, where they were detained and interrogated by the *Guardia Civil*, a feared militarised police force that enjoyed an almost unlimited power in Spain at that time. Although they were later released without charge, the reason for such harsh treatment had to do with the presence in the area of active groups of *maquis*, the defeated Republican soldiers who kept fighting the fascist regime of General Franco using guerrilla methods at the end of the Spanish Civil War. Back in 1944, a force of four to seven thousand Spanish *maquis* – most of whom had also fought against the Germans in the French resistance – crossed the Pyrenees and occupied the Aran Valley in Spain. Their goal was not to progress beyond the valley but to consolidate their position so that by the time the Germans had been totally defeated, the Allies would have to turn their eyes to Spain.

It was also hoped that the invasion would contribute to producing a popular uprising against Franco, something that never happened. After three weeks of occupation, the *maquis* were forced to retreat back to France, where they were disarmed by the new de Gaulle government. In the following years, small groups of combatants continued to cross the border to commit acts of sabotage, and for that reason the *Guardia Civil* maintained a strong presence in the mountain passes of the Pyrenees. At a time when climbing and mountaineering were activities mostly unheard of in Spain, finding foreigners like Donald McKean and his companions in the proximity of the border was naturally viewed by the *Guardia Civil* as something extremely suspicious.

Surprising as this information was, I was even more amazed when he told me that he had published a description of his adventure in the 1950 edition of the Oxford Mountaineering Journal, the same edition that contained the obituaries of William, Ian and James. I had seen this article the second time I visited the OUMC library, but not for a second had I made the connection between the Donald McKean who authored the article and Ian – at that point I didn't even know that Ian had a brother.

The most memorable moment of the afternoon, though, took

Above: The whole OUMC group, pictured together in Orsières for the last time. They had arrived from Courmayeur on July 15, ten days before the accident. Morale was low, as it had snowed copiously for the last three days.

Below: Zermatt in 1947, depicted on postcard sent by William Bell to a friend after he and Ian had climbed the Matterhorn.

Above: The morning of July 24th, 1948, before leaving for the Matterhorn. In the preceding days the team had done some good climbs, and morale was high once again.

Below: James Ogilvie (second from left), Ian McKean (centre) and William Bell (second from right) the day before the accident on the Matterhorn.

place almost at the end of our visit, when Donald showed us an old picture. In it, five boys dressed in mountaineering outfits were happily smiling at the photographer, all of them leaning on long ice axes as if they were dancers in the *Top Hat* musical movie, leaning on their walking sticks, waiting for Fred Astaire to make his appearance on the film set. I immediately recognised the man who was sitting in front of me. In the picture, Donald McKean was on the far left, the tallest of the group, looking slightly bashful with his thick spectacles, an incipient beard, and wearing what to all appearances was a too-loose military coat. I also recognised William Bell, the second from the right, with the same boyish smile as in the portrait in his book. This time, however, he didn't seem to be imprisoned by a tie or Brylcreemed hair. On the contrary, he looked amused and relaxed. "He was a natural leader, with a lot of charisma," Donald told us, when I pointed at William. Indeed, that was what the body language of the group seemed to indicate: even though he was not in the central position in the picture, William was slightly ahead of the rest, which drew the eye to him. The one in the centre of the picture, immediately behind William, was his brother Ian, Donald told us, with long, wavy blonde hair, looking confidently straight at the camera, with snow goggles hanging round his neck. James Ogilvie stood between the McKean brothers. He looked quite composed, with small eyes, a warm smile on his face, and what appeared to be a strong physique. The last member of the group, on the right side, was Ted Simpson.

All of them carried climbing ropes on their shoulders and they seemed to be full of life. All of them exuded youth, and an aura of immortality could almost be perceived around them. The picture was taken on 24 July of 1948, the day before the accident.

14. In Hell as it is in Heaven

More than kisses, letters mingle souls
John Donne

George Orwell is often quoted as saying that 'Writing a book is a horrible, exhausting struggle, like a long bout of some painful illness. One would never undertake such a thing if one were not driven on by some demon whom one can neither resist nor understand.' The list of famous authors bitterly moaning about the misery of writing is endless, but the most inspired one was Gene Fowler, an American journalist, author and dramatist. He is remembered, among other things, for saying that 'Writing is easy. All you do is sit staring at a blank sheet of paper until drops of blood form on your forehead.'

Yes, writing is hard. So hard that, from time to time, you find yourself questioning whether all the effort you are putting in is worth it. One of these 'mini-crises' occurred for me a few hours after leaving the McKeans. It was almost midnight and Marian and I were still at Edinburgh airport, our flight hugely delayed. After what had been an intense weekend, we were both physically and mentally drained. The worst part was to know that, after arriving at Luton, we would still have a long drive home, only to wake up barely four hours later to start what promised to be a tough working week at the office. I was particularly concerned for her: after all, this was my own personal journey. Because of it, she was making plenty of sacrifices as well, including many nights when she went to sleep alone, and numerous weekends where I left her by herself because I had to finish this or that chapter. I was considering all of this when she looked at me and admitted that meeting the Ogilvies and the McKeans had been some of the most precious experiences of her life.

Yes, writing is hard. However, researching this book, looking for information, exploring dusty bookshelves, talking to people, and above all, coming to know the Ogilvie and McKean families – that was a wonderful adventure as well as a privilege. For that reason, looking back, I can't feel anything but an immense gratitude for every single moment I devoted to it since I first saw the tombstone of William, Ian and James in Zermatt. That feeling of being part of something extraordinary was once again confirmed when I finally had the opportunity to go through the material that David and Donald had kindly entrusted me with.

The selection of letters that James had sent to his family whilst at school, and again during his time in the army, for example, were extremely useful for learning new details about his life: things such as his dislike for Rugby, or that he had spent two terms in Balliol before joining the army at Christmas 1943. They also confirmed that James had indeed rejected a commission so he could fight in Holland alongside the men with whom he had shared basic training. Only once the war was over did he take up the commission, passing out from officer training as Senior Under-Officer with the Sword of Honour. He was sent to India first and Burma later. Burma in particular was a tough destination, with anti-British sentiment running high after the war. James was awarded the Burma Star for his service against the *Mujahedeen* guerrillas in Arakan district, who wanted to merge this part of Burma into East Pakistan, now Bangladesh. According to the document, James was one of the last British officers to leave Burma.

The letters also provided me with plenty of evidence of James's virtues: his sense of honour, his courage, his humble character, his love for music and the close affection he felt for his family – 'how I remember playing the oboe with my dear father years and years ago; little did I see then how happy I was'. In the letters I found someone with an enormous capacity to mock himself; someone with often mordant points of view on army rules; someone with remarkably shrewd opinions; someone who was able to wistfully look back and part-fearfully, part-joyously look forward. Above all, he was someone with a natural curiosity for the world around him and the people who inhabited it, regardless of their class and origin.

In a letter from Rugby at the end of 1942, James evoked his afternoon bicycle rides during the previous summer as 'a happy time, an escape into a lovely world of simple, kind folk with a good-humoured timelessness about them'. During these rides he would often embark on conversations with strangers, 'like the man who saved up the proceeds of his village store to go to India to look at their stained glass, or the farmer's wife who wrote books without a thought of trying to get them published'. Reading his letters, it is easy to appreciate that James always felt more at ease among farmers, shop-owners, and factory workers, than among his peers at Rugby. No surprise, then, that he decided to reject the commission: it was clear that he would rather share laughs with other fellow troopers in the mess tent of the barracks, than spend time with prig officers at the regimental club.

Reading James's letters was a joy. His prose was succinct but agile; clinical but warm; to-the-point but evocative. Above all, honest and humorous. Without any doubt, he was a natural born writer – one of the few chosen ones who possess the elusive ability to transport the reader to wherever he is and help him see whatever he is actually seeing.

Often I have stood by the open window of my dormitory and looked out. Mist would be there, perhaps, and out of it loom the great elms, and, from above, there is the rich, cool light of the moon. I have seemed to hear the music of

the stars, coming down with the moonbeams through miles
of space and years of time to me. Then you hear the hum of
conversation from the other dormitories. Someone is telling
a story. A laugh. Then more steady talk. More laughter, gay,
wide, open laughter for the very joy of living. Someone is
talking about the things he loves and the people he loves.
They all seem so much older now and greater and wiser
than their faces would suggest. One by one stop talking; the
conversation flares up for a bit, then dies out completely.
There is a softer mumble, rising and falling in the cool air.
A far laugh. Then it stops. And suddenly you realise how
cold it is.

One of the most beautiful fragments in James's letters is when he
describes a family of Dutch farmers he became friends with during
the winter of 1944, the last one of the war.

Who are these people, the Gerritsen? About the most perfect
family in the world. They are like everyone around here,
peasants or Boers. That is to say, they live on the land and
for the land; they have six pigs, two sheep, a horse, some hens
and a byre-full of cows who stand there all day thinking
cowy. 'Papa', so we call him, is like any other Boer: hard-
working, honest, a good father to his six children. But
he reads; he has a full bookcase in his parlour which he
showed me, some on travel. 'Mama' is a great character: in
the twenties she went as nursemaid to a little boy with his
mother from Amsterdam to the Dutch Indies, and you can
imagine what an effect such a world tour had on a peasant
girl. It has made up in experience what she lacked, perhaps,
in education and it's clear that she kept her eyes open during
the whole trip.

James later gives a brief description of the children of the family.
When he comes to the youngest one, he says, "Bernhardt is all

that a one-year-old should be, with his eyes that ask a thousand questions of the world, and are content to get no answer, his chubby fingers which explore whatever they can catch, and little mouth, always just open, expecting an eternal wonder and interest in life." The most interesting part in this letter comes when he tries to explain the reasons why he has grown so fond of the Gerritsen family.

> Why is it that we should have grown, not to like them, but to love them? Is it just that, being soldiers, any home has a rich appeal? I don't think so. In our travels to and from I have been in many Dutch homes and I look back on them all with very happy memories; yet I realise that this is something different. Principally it is, I think, because of a series of quite small things: the look of infinite gratitude in Papa's eye when we gave each of his children a bar of chocolate; the discipline but complete happiness of the children; the cleanliness of everything in the house; the love of Papa for Mama; the saying of the long family grace after the evening meal; the sight of children lying asleep, some in cots, others in beds, while the proud parents showed us around on tip-toe, with the light of an oil lamp; the tone of voice with which they beg us to come again. Nothing the English do is anything but good to them; over and over again they say 'you have saved our children'. They have nothing beyond the bare necessities of life. In spite of it all, they are utterly dignified and without bitterness; they have forgotten what is to have new clothes but they contrive to keep smart those that they have, and they have not forgotten what it is to love.

What amazed me most about James's war letters was how he refused to let hatred fill his heart. 'There is far more hate talk in the press than at the front,' he writes in April 1945. Like a real traveller, he looks for whatever he has in common with the people he encounters, to a point where the sense of otherness very often vanishes completely in his correspondence.

'Among the ruins of buildings, you often find photographs of German soldiers. It is comforting in this world, where we are told to hate each other, as though we were beings with essential differences, to see how similar the subjects of those photographs are,' he writes in March 1945, only to add a few days later that, 'After the Dutch, we have found the Germans most like us and Germany most like England and, speaking for myself, I have felt more at ease among them than among the French.'

However, he sometimes feels doubts and wonders whether things would be easier if he were a better hater, if he could see things in black and white as, in his opinion, Americans often do. 'I believe that the wrath of the Americans is colossal and, from experience, I know that the anger of the Canadians is hardly less so', he writes. However, James's compassion for those who suffer, no matter whether they are Dutch or German civilians, or Eastern slave-workers, always prevails. It was comforting to see how his sense of right and wrong was not at all destroyed or dampened by the war. 'I believe that Germany is guilty and they must not be allowed to start another war. But when I see the under-fives looking so sadly at us, I feel it would be wrong not to give them my chocolate; and when an old woman, seeing us cooking in the street, invites us to cook on her stove and eat at her table, I know that it is only right to wash her dishes for her. Only the very young and the very old are left and, thank God, there is hardly any soldier in the Second Army who would not respect and know them. Non-fraternisation, forsooth', he writes with irony in May 1945 about the non-fraternisation policy promoted by the Allied commanders.

A new letter sent by him a few days later, on 8 May 1945, Victory in Europe Day, contains a delightful imaginary dialogue between him and General Dwight Eisenhower, the Supreme Commander of the Allied Forces in Europe, in relation to the non-fraternisation policy that had been distributed to all Allied soldiers:

- *Gee, I sure guess you are nuts, or haven't you read my little dinky book?*

- *'Yes, General,' I answer.*

- *Page 27. 'The likeness if it exists at all is only skin deep. The deeper you dig into the German character, the more you realise how different they are from us. So don't be taken by first impressions.'*

- *No, General.*

- *Furthermore, on page 4 is written: 'Don't be taken in by surface resemblance between the Germans and ourselves.'*

- *No, General. May a buddy speak?*

- *Yes, I guess so.*

- *General, I admit I have noticed a resemblance. So have others. I admit that in two years', ten years', twenty years' time I may have discovered the resemblance to be only 'skin deep'. Or I may not. Only our own experience can answer that for us. Meanwhile –*

- *Shut up.*

- *Yes, General.*

At which point I, Trooper Ogilvie, wake up to find myself imprisoned for life and stripped of my rights as a citizen, for the Americans take their beliefs seriously.

★

The letters sent by James from India and Burma between 1946 and the summer of 1947, however, provide a different perspective on him. In them, James appears more relaxed, more settled down; at times, he even seems to enjoy the order and routine of his life in the army. The contrast with the letters from Holland and Germany is evident in many ways. During the war, James's correspondence shows the continuous process of self-examination he is going through: a process during which he questions his feelings towards everything that surrounds him, from the suffering of civilians to the instructions he receives from his superiors. Above all, he questions his feelings towards the war; many times he seems to be torn between the repulsion he feels by war's catastrophic effects, in particular over the most vulnerable (elderly and children), and the conviction of believing in the righteousness of its cause.

In contrast, the letters from India and Burma are more descriptive, with less room for introspection. In them, James becomes more of a spectator: still curious and amazed by whatever he sees, but also managing to keep a certain distance between him and his environment. As is natural, the issues he talks about are more diverse, from how District Offices could provide cheap accommodation to young hikers or travellers – 'many of them are superbly situated, and I could think of few better places to spend a holiday' – to the wonders that nature offers to him – 'The buck reached the hedge and leapt into the air. It was a rare and beautiful sight: chest thrown forward, head thrown back, rear legs thin and straight behind him, forelegs arched, the whole body delicate and light and yet infinitely strong. For a moment, he seemed to hang there, poised in the air against the back-cloth of sunset.'

Not surprisingly, as James was in India while the country was heading towards independence, he talks frequently about politics too. Both Nehru and Jinnah, the first prime ministers of the independent India and Pakistan respectively, are defined as 'political jugglers'. And of Nehru in particular, he says that 'his exploits are surely a subject worthy both of the pomp of Verdi, and the satire of Gilbert and Sullivan', the authors of the comic operas *The Pirates of Penzance* and *The Mikado*. However, as in his years back in England, it is the life of common people that really attracts James's attention. Of all the subjects of the Empire, he feels particularly impressed by Sikhs, who he said 'would have admired the same sort of men as Homer admired – Ajax and Hector and Achilles and Agamemnon – and for the same sort of reasons, particularly their courage and prowess as warriors.'

In his letters from India and Burma, James shows the same sense of decency – of what is right and wrong – as in those written during the war. In one of them, he is incensed by a malaise that most British suffer and that he calls 'a snobbishness of blood', as a result of which 'no matter how efficient or competent you may be … if you don't come from the right family, and the right school, you are only second best'. To illustrate his point, he gives the example of a Lieutenant Kirby, who 'has won more scholarships and bursaries than most of us would expect to pick up in a lifetime, and will almost certainly get his First at Cambridge; but, what does that avail a chap who speaks with a Midlands accent?'

In a separate letter, he talks about an incident involving his Commanding Officer, Captain Sidhu, an Indian who 'spent fourteen years in the ranks before being commissioned'. James always talks about him with great affection and respect because of his leadership capacity and competence. However, other British officers evidently thought otherwise, as James illustrates.

> *When I reached Mingaladon with the advance party, one of the first things the Colonel of the Gurkhas asked me was 'Who is your O.C.?'*
> - *Captain Sidhu.*
> - *What, an Indian?*
> - *Yes.*
> - *What is the army coming to when you have to serve under a Wog?*

James was more than furious at these words.

★

The *pièce de résistance* in James's correspondence is a letter written on 18 April 1948, to his uncle, Dr Robert Hardie, who at that time was practising in Kuala Lumpur, Malaysia – and what a letter it is! More than fifteen pages long, in it James describes in full detail a two-week trip to the Scottish central Highlands together with William and Ian, a practice for their climbing holiday in the Alps the next summer. A key part of the letter's value resides in the fact that it shows James in his purest form: already having left behind the shadows of the war, and finally liberated from the army's straitjacket, he is more relaxed and funnier than ever. During the whole trip, James exudes a boundless passion for everything surrounding him and he seems as happy as he probably ever was. More importantly for me, James offers a wonderful, rich description of William and Ian and his relationship with them.

The letter, which begins with James's normal display of modesty ('I ought to warn you that we achieved nothing spectacular, that the distances covered were modest, and that the times we took will horrify you'), is addressed to Uncle Robert, to whom James credits his growing passion for mountains. 'Your tales and your maps shook my fervour,' he writes, making reference to Uncle Robert's past as a hill-walker and climber. 'The speed of your Glen Feshie walk is, of course, still treasured among the legends of the family,' he adds. However, that was not James's only reason to write to him. 'Dare one hope that talk of your old haunts will do something to kindle nostalgia in you and lead you homeward?' As in the rest of his correspondence, James never makes any effort to conceal his love and warmth for his family.

Then he describes William and Ian.

> *William is a scholar of English at Merton College, a High Church Tory of 18th century vintage, a poet who has succeeded in publishing a couple of books in as many years*

(I can't understand a word of them!), a native of Derby. I met him last Christmas at a meet of the OUMC in the Lake District. It was my first venture on rock and it was inglorious. Time and time again I had to be hauled from above and pushed from below, and after dangling on a rope for all of an afternoon in drenching rain I was heard to utter the shocking heresy that all sane folk would prefer to take the path up Great Gable instead of crawling up the buttresses of the north face. As William is a climber of some skill and experience one must assume (a) he never happened to be on the same rope as I during the week in the Lakes; and (b) that news of my blasphemy never reached him.

The other member of the party was Ian McKean. Ian is the bright boy of my year at Balliol; he got a first in Mods and is well set for a first in Greats. He is as zealous a Nonconformist as William is an Anglican; while William is a Tory, Ian is an ardent Socialist. Indeed he is the chairman of the University Labour Club and as such acted as the PM's host when he came down for the weekend last term. He has not quite as much experience of hills as William – that's to say, he has been climbing for about eighteen months, including a season in Switzerland.

We were a motley party, then, and you can imagine that our meetings before the tour, to decide on routes and organise details, were colourful and at times anarchical. In these early stages it was Ian who made the whole trip possible. William was inclined to bristle with wild plans involving a month of trekking across the more deserted regions of Scotland until we reached Skye and I could do little more than try to learn from maps something of a part of the world of which I knew nothing. But Ian planned like a true Socialist; thanks to him, food was dispatched hither and thither to await our arrival; accommodation was arranged for every stage and one sort of time-table prepared.

163

Is it possible to say more in just a few paragraphs? I doubt it. With a great sense of humour – I love William's portrayal as 'a Tory of eighteenth century vintage' – James masterfully describes the contrasting characters of his friends: the Tory and the Socialist, the Anglican and the Nonconformist. William the day-dreamer, who aims to plan the expedition to Scotland as if they are trying to rediscover the sources of the river Nile, in contrast with Ian, the pragmatic, who instead deals efficiently with all the problems of the trip.

After they arrive in Crianlarich, a village that bills itself as the gateway to the Highlands, it becomes evident that William has adopted the position of leader of the group, not only because of his superior climbing skills, but also because of his enthusiastic personality. "We had not climbed a thousand feet on Ben More before William noticed a cliff, and in spite of our mild protest he piloted Ian and I towards it," James writes about their first day in Scotland. However, William's leadership is on occasions more theoretical than real. In fact, Ian and James sometimes mutiny against it, as happened when they tried to descend Creise, at the eastern end of Glen Coe, following a route that William had suggested. 'He vowed that he knew the way off it,' but soon, Ian and James found themselves in a particularly dangerous gully, 'as rotten as any in Scotland where a fall seemed only a matter of time.'

> When we reached the bottom we waited for William. No sign. We shouted. No answer. We waited for ten minutes and got exceedingly cold. Then we started to climb up the gully once more, and in the course of the climb I dislodged a small mountain that missed Ian by a couple of feet, and a little later a solid-looking hand-hold, on which Ian had been relying, simply disintegrated, and for an appalling space of time he dangled from a tuft of heather while his feet pawed the bottom of the gully in search of something

to grip on. But all was well, and we reached the top to find that William had lost his spectacles. The day before we spent twenty minutes returning to the top of Buachaille Etive Mor in search of the self-same spectacles, so that we had little love for them or their owner by the time we were ready, once more, to slither our way to the bottom of the gully. Let me assure you that there are easier and wiser routes off Creise than the gully on the north-west face.

Not surprisingly, later that day, "when we reached the Etive river, William muttered something about there being a bucket bridge a mile downstream but Ian and I were now sceptical of any hypothesis William might advance."

At other times, William's suggestions are simply too eccentric to be taken seriously, such as his proposal to bathe in a small stream near the Youth Hostel where they were staying. "Ian and I put our fingers in the burn and decided against it, to the astonishment of the leader who proceeded to submerge himself in it. Mercifully the chill of the water rendered him speechless, but while drying himself afterwards he boldly asserted that he had enjoyed his plunge," James writes with a small note of sarcasm in his words.

Despite some disagreements now and then, quite often caused by William's colourful character, the relationship between the three boys is one based on affection, respect and camaraderie. "William had that greatest of all virtues in a leader: consideration for those coming after. And when one's turn came to climb, one knew that William's stance above was firm, and found that he was enduring one's own delays with exemplary patience and kindness," James writes about him. On another day, trekking from Beinn Fhada to Bidean nam Bian, the group is caught by a terrible blizzard, which "soon reduced visibility to under ten yards, and before long afterwards made it impossible for us to open our eyes". Reflecting on the difficult circumstances in which they found themselves,

James says, "I give full marks to William and Ian who between them navigated our party to the shoulder of An t-Sron, which was little short of heroic in that blizzard." The day ended, 'as such days should', round a blazing fire, with a mug of steaming tea, and talk of hills.

The letter is full of rich descriptions of the places they visit, "I don't remember seeing such a noble sunset; there was a touch of frost in the evening which seemed to give the air a cutting cleanness; the silhouette of Ben Challum stood poised against the glowing redness of the sky, and all the while the sun dropped towards the horizon." He also describes their accommodation in exquisite detail, "Do you know Lagangarbh? It is primitive but perfectly adequate; you draw your water from a burn only twenty yards from the front door. There are oil lamps for light and oil stoves for cooking, and a large grate which does its best to dry your clothes for you even if it doesn't quite succeed." Food, which apparently is much better than whatever they had back at the university, is also a common topic in James's letters: "Yesterday's meal is a proof that compared with England, Scotland is a land flowing with milk and honey."

Naturally, he also provides plentiful accounts of the climbs they make: "Our ascent of Nevis was a cheerless affair from start to finish. We chose the southeast ridge, as the cliffs were plastered with snow and the gullies were dangerously soft. My impressions of the highest mountain in the British Isles were of cold and mist; there was nothing whatever to see and nothing whatever to enjoy. I just remember the wind, which took a mean delight in wrapping our sodden clothes with a peculiarly shivering blast."

It is during one of their climbs, on Sgorr nam Fiannaidh, when the only accident of the trip occurred: William fell when a snow bridge collapsed under his weight, 'He got up at once, apparently unhurt, but he had wrenched his knee and it gave trouble the following days.'

However, the most interesting descriptions provided by James are neither of mountains nor climbing feats, but of some of the people they find on their way. Of Mrs Lorimer, who looks after a hut not far from Coylumbridge, James says, "She is, I swear, the salt of the earth. Nothing was too much trouble for her. When we had cleared her table of food she laid before us; when we arrived late for supper or asked for an early breakfast, she did not wince or subdue her kindliness. Towards William and his knee she was positively motherly and he revelled in her attentions like a spoilt child. Before we left, she gave us each two dozen eggs, which our respective homes voted the most precious present received for many a long day. Let the name of Mrs Lorimer be held in reverence and honour."

However, James is much less kind when he describes their encounter with members of the Cambridge University Mountaineering Club one night, at a hut.

> Within half an hour war had been declared. We found them arrogant and loud-mouthed; we felt that their coarse jokes didn't sound funny in Crianlarich Youth Hostel (and they clearly embarrassed a couple of girls who were eating their supper in the corner) and we judged that their yarns of exploits in the Alps were at least improbable. What irritated us more than anything else was the running commentary which their leader delivered on the cooking operations. His party, you see, were sitting round one of the tables and he was at the other end of the room cooking them some pancakes. It is true that we were waiting for the stove ourselves, and may therefore have been uncharitable and intolerant, but we felt that his dissertation about the temperature of the fat, his explanation of the difficulties involved in tossing a pancake, his reminiscences of pancakes he had made in Switzerland, his comparisons of his pancakes with other people's pancakes, his imprecations when the pancakes got

*burned, his exhortation to eat the pancakes while they were
hot, his panegyric of pancakes in general and his pancakes in
particular – all this, I say, struck us as irrelevant and drove
us into a frenzy, not least because it was shouted fortissimo
across the room. Luckily they retired to bed not longer after
the last pancake had been served with the usual voluble
explanations; whether this was from indigestion or honest
exertion was not clear. Then William cooked some soup, Ian
some bacon and I some potatoes, and we ended the day in a
benign mode.*

The letter, unfortunately, finishes with a reminder of their penniless
situation, the ultimate reason why they decided not to hire a guide
in Zermatt to climb the Matterhorn. "The trek was over. Just as
well, too: we had two and ninepence half-penny between us and
that, as William mournfully remarked, was not even enough to
buy us the wherewithal to celebrate the end."

Driven by curiosity, and after reading James's letter to his uncle,
Robert Hardie, I looked for references about him on the Internet.
Honestly, I was not expecting to find anything particularly relevant.
As many other times before, I was wrong.

After reading medicine at Edinburgh University, Robert had
qualified as a doctor in 1935, and in 1937 he was offered a
partnership in a medical practice in Kuala Lumpur, Malaysia. In
1939 he was commissioned as a medical officer in the 3rd Malayan
Volunteer Field Ambulance. When Singapore fell to the Japanese
forces in February 1942, he became a prisoner of war. James's uncle
was one of the more than 61,000 Allied prisoners of war who were
forced by the Japanese to work on the notorious Burma-Siam
railway. More than 16,000 of them died from sickness, exhaustion
and malnutrition, an average of one victim for every 28 yards of

track. One of the best war movies ever made, *The Bridge on the River Kwai*, with the unforgettable Alec Guinness in the role of Colonel Nicholson, was based on these events.

For three years, Robert Hardie and other medical officials in the prison camps along the railway worked in appalling conditions to stem the ravages of beriberi, cholera, malaria, and other tropical diseases, often using surgical instruments improvised out of scrap metal and with totally inadequate supplies of drugs and dressings. Throughout this period, he kept a diary, which he managed to conceal from the Japanese, despite numerous searches. The diary was published in 1983 by the Imperial War Museum with the title of *The Burma-Siam Railway: The Secret Diary of Dr Robert Hardie 1942–1945*. The book, which vividly conveys the hardships, monotony and humiliations of life in the overcrowded camps along the course of the so-called 'Railway of Death', not only makes incredible reading but, more importantly, stands as a testimony to the resilience and courage of the British prisoners of war in the Far East.

23 March 1943

I just got back to Wan Tow Kien after two days at Chungkai. I went down accompanying a party of 110 sick. There were mostly beriberi, pellagra and dysentery. Many of them were in a desperate state after their journey down by barge the day before. We left in the early morning. The Japanese allowed one lorry to make just one trip to the station, which is about three kilometres from the camp, with ten sick men who couldn't walk. Others who couldn't walk had to be helped by parties of fit men who carried them on their backs or sitting on their clasped hands, in relays. It was an exhausting journey even over that distance. It was hard work for the fit men but they did very well – even so it was absolutely prostrating for these fearfully sick men, some of them mere skeletons, gaunt, fleshless and despairing. It was a blazing hot day. When we got to the station, the Jap guards compelled us to load the helpless sick into open trucks standing in the sun, and there they lay for an hour before the train started. We had only our water bottles. When we reached Wang Lang station we again stood in the sun for an hour.

Many times along my quest I found that not only were William, Ian and James extraordinary men, but they were also surrounded by extraordinary people. Robert Hardie certainly was one of them.

15. Ancestors and descendants

Family is not an important thing. It is everything.
Michael J. Fox

The other issue that occupied my mind in the days immediately after returning from Scotland was something that both Donald and David had asked me, "Did you find any relatives of William Bell?" My answer had been negative, simply because I hadn't even looked for them. The truth was that I hadn't looked for the McKeans or the Ogilvies either. It was they who had, somehow, managed to find me. In theory, lightning does not strike twice but reality had proved me wrong. Could it possibly be third time lucky? There was only one way to find out – I would once again have to put on my detective hat and try to locate William's family.

I don't watch a lot of television, but one of my favourite programmes is *Who Do You Think You Are?* Every week, and with the support of experts in genealogy, a celebrity traces his or her family tree, which often results in interesting and sometimes shocking discoveries about their family's history. For example, one of the guests once found out that his great-great-great grandfather had been a slave master as well as the owner of large sugar plantations in Jamaica. The guest didn't know anything about this ugly side of his family and, needless to say, he was completely and utterly mortified. I also recall how people such as Jerry Springer and Natasha Kaplinsky, so often composed and self-controlled, cried inconsolably like babies when they found out about the fate of their relatives in Eastern Europe during the Holocaust. The programme is sponsored by a website dedicated to providing support to those who wish to track down their ancestors. It was while watching an advertisement for this company that it occurred to me that perhaps I could use their services to locate William's relatives. After all, I had nothing to lose and no better idea of how to do it.

The genealogy site functions in a quite straightforward and user-friendly way: it contains millions of scanned documents including birth, death and marriage records from all parishes across Britain and Ireland; data from the UK census of 1891, 1901 and 1911; military records; last wills; telephone guides, *et cetera*. All you have to do is introduce as much information as possible about the ancestor you want to trace, such as the name, date and place of birth, occupation, and in a few seconds you will have a list of all potential matches on your screen. In a way, it is like fishing – you cast your fishing rod and once a potential match is identified, you just start reeling in the line. You can also build up a family tree using the information obtained, and the site automatically looks for correlation between your tree and those created by other users. Although I didn't know it when I signed up, this particular tool would play a priceless role in my search.

An old Chinese proverb says, 'Even a journey of a thousand miles begins with a single step.' For me, that initial step was the information contained in Merton's registry: according to which William was the son of Dr M. C. Bell, of Shardlow, Derbyshire. Without giving too much thought to it, I naturally took for granted that Dr M. C. Bell would be William's father. However, according to the census, between 1910 and 1945 there seemed to be no male doctor in the UK who could respond to those initials and name. The college registry, I found out later, contained a small error that had gone undetected. It was insignificant, but because of it my quest was rendered fruitless for almost seventy-two hours.

Had I cross-checked the registry with other sources, such as the letter which William's father had sent to Ian Davie on 2 August 1948, after the latter had written offering his condolences to the family in the aftermath of the accident, the error could have been spotted earlier. The note was correctly signed by Dr Harry C. Bell; that is, H. C. Bell rather than by Dr M. C. Bell. So, did the registry contain a typo or they were two different people? The answer surfaced when I checked the UK Medical Registers 1859-1959 again. There I found, just one above the other, the names of H. C. Bell and M. C. Bell – Harry Cooke Bell and Mary Caroline Bell. They were William's father *and* mother, her maiden name being Lindsay. The fact that they shared the same middle initial 'C' is what probably created the confusion at Merton registry, as the norm at that time for this kind of university records was to mention only the name of the student's father, rather than his mother.

For both parents to be doctors, as in the case of William, was extremely unusual in the early twentieth century. Back then not many women had access to university studies. In addition, for those who eventually entered university, medicine was not an obvious choice. Mary Caroline obtained her degree at Queen's University in Belfast in April 1922. It is possible that her decision to study medicine was inspired by the tireless and devoted work of doctors and nurses on the Western Front during World War I, where they saved thousands of lives. The shortage of young men in Britain as a result of the carnage caused by the war facilitated the access of women, like Mary Caroline, to what until then was a professional career mostly restricted to men.

Also, according to the information provided by the website, William's father had died relatively young, in 1958, only ten years after the accident on the Matterhorn, at the age of 64. That reminded me of James's father, who had also died not long after his son's death. The parallels between the Bell and Ogilvie families didn't end there, as Mary Caroline Bell, like Mary Ogilvie, had led a long and fruitful professional life. While the mother of James had a fulfilling career at Oxford University, William's mother practised

173

medicine for almost half a century. In 1993, and at the age of 94, she died in Derby, where she had lived most of her life.

The records offered me other useful information about the Bell family: for example, that Harry and Mary Caroline had another son, Robert, who was born in 1925, a year after William. However, this younger brother had died in 1995, which meant that I would never meet him, as I had done with the brothers of James and Ian. I would be lying if I said I was not disappointed. The site did, however, also indicate that Robert had a daughter, Brigid Bell, who according to my calculations should be in her mid-fifties or early sixties. Not all was lost; should I find her, I was confident that she would be able to provide me with plenty of information about her uncle. Even though she may not have known him personally, I had a hunch that William's presence in the oral tradition of the family would have been quite strong.

Then I hit a brick wall.

The website is indeed a fantastic place for anyone who wants to unearth their family history. Getting access to information about people who may still be alive, however, is a completely different matter. In fact, it is completely forbidden by the Data Protection Act. Otherwise, sites like this one could be used, for example, by criminal gangs to get valuable, sensitive data about potential victims. It was evident that I had reached a dead end. It is true that along this journey I had been in difficult situations before, from which no exit could be easily visualised at the time, but this time it was different: this dead end was one directly enforced by the law.

Like a castaway desperately scanning the horizon in the hope of finding a saviour ship, I spent the next couple of days searching the net for any trace of Brigid Bell – any lead, anything at all that could take me to her. I found absolutely nothing.

Then something magical happened. Again. When I thought that all hope was lost, I added William's grandparents from his mother's side, Caroline West and Robert Lindsay, to the family tree that I had created. A small green leaf started flickering intensely and growing on the screen, and a little window said, "We found hints with potential matches from one public member tree." I followed the link provided, and a family tree, much larger and more detailed than mine, appeared before my eyes. William's grandfather Robert Lindsay was the connection between them.

The new tree had two main branches, the Lindsays on one side, and the Bells on the other. The latter was identical to mine with a notable difference – Brigid Bell appeared under the name of Brigid Hamilton-Jones. It could only mean one thing: Brigid Bell and Brigid Hamilton-Jones were the same person, before and after getting married. Even more important than that was the fact that Brigid herself appeared to be the person who had created the family tree, and her email address was shown at the bottom of the page. In a fraction of a second, with a mouse click, I had killed two birds with one stone; I had got both the present name of William's niece and her contact details. In my already long list of serendipitous happenings, this new one immediately acquired a prominent position.

There was a small setback, though, as the site also indicated that she had not logged in for more than four years. In short, it was possible that her email account was not active any more. I searched the net again, this time using her married surname. Bits and pieces of her surfaced, scattered here and there – a blog she created with the last entry written more than three years ago; a couple of messages posted in 2002 on an American forum; and a profile on Facebook with no picture, no messages on the wall, and no visible signs of activity. For a moment, I even feared that something could have happened to her at some point after 2009.

However, I had come too far to be dissuaded by this possibility. So, that day I prepared a detailed email for her explaining who I was and why I was interested in her uncle, which I sent to the address that appeared on the website. I also sent it to what seemed to be her Facebook account. As a final resort, I talked to the customer services department of the genealogy website. When I had completed my subscription I had to provide contact details, including a postal address as well as mobile and landline phone numbers. I didn't expect them to give me that information for Brigid. Instead, my hope was that they could transmit a message to her on my behalf, something that they were allowed to do, explaining why I wanted to get in contact. The person who I talked to, Richard Coplen, could not have been more kind and he happily promised me he would do it.

After all these comings and goings, there was nothing to do but wait. Three days later, I got the following email:

Dear Mateo,

Thank you for your message. As you can imagine I was very surprised to find that someone is writing a book about my uncle! I wanted to take a couple of days to think about my response and also to inform other members of the family. Could you explain what has prompted you to write the book? I do have some photos and of course can tell you a lot about my father, but I never met William. Here is a bit of what I do know.

My father was born in 1925 and died in 1995. He was just 16 months younger than William. I gather that they fought a lot when they were small boys! They were very different physically. William was quite short and my father was a bit over 6 foot. My father had quite poor eyesight and didn't particularly enjoy sports at school. I remember him telling me that he had broken 13 bones before he left school (that might be an exaggeration)! Both boys were gifted academically. I'm a bit vague on William's academic career – possibly you know more than me, but of course he was a student at Merton College Oxford.

Both boys went to Epsom College (a boys' public boarding school) which specialized in the education of doctors' sons. My father followed his parents into the medical profession. He went to St Mary's Hospital Paddington in 1943 or 44 (I think). He met my mother at St Mary's (she was a nurse) and they were married in 1949. My father was doing his National Service at the time and they immediately went to live in Austria. After finishing National Service, my father joined his parents in their Shardlow general practice and my parents lived with them. At some point after that (my brother will know when) my father rejoined the army and he then served in the RAMC until he retired at the age of 60. My father's specialism in the army was Army Health (equivalent to Public Health, i.e. mainly preventative medicine).

I hope this information is useful. Do ask any questions that occur to you. If you have scanned version of the photos perhaps you could send them to me and then I can see if I have any that you don't have.

I look forward to hearing from you again.

Best wishes

Brigid

Someone may assume that, after so many exciting discoveries, this was just one more in the long list of surprises and happy happenings that the quest has brought with it – a kind of 'another-day-at-the-Matterhorn-office' moment. It wasn't. For me, getting news from the closest living relative of William Bell was as electrifying as when, while in Mauritius, I first learned about the existence of Donald McKean and David Ogilvic. Perhaps even more so.

When my little 'detective-esque' affair began, I did not set any objectives or targets. I never told myself that I had to find anything specific. As a result, every new piece of information unearthed was a bonus, a joyful and unique occasion that deserved to be celebrated. Yet, getting in contact with William's niece was truly special. In a way, the circle was completed now: I had got as close to William, Ian and James as possible. It was something that, when I first saw their tombstone in Zermatt a few months earlier, knowing only their names, I would have deemed simply inconceivable.

I felt as if I had reached the summit of my own mountain. Of course, there were many loose ends that I still needed to check and many potential sources of information that needed to be verified, but I had truly reached the summit.

16. The descent

That evening I wrote a longer email to Brigid explaining everything that had happened since I had come across William, Ian and James in the cemetery at Zermatt, including the discoveries I had made in the OUMC library, the acquisition by Merton of William's letters and documents, and, of course, my meetings with Donald and David in Scotland. Finally, I forwarded to her a couple of emails that I had exchanged with Stephen Venables, in which I sketched the structure and content of the book. Five minutes later, Brigid replied:

> *Dear Mateo,*
>
> *I haven't finished reading everything, but I had to write back and say that I used to know Stephen Venables! We both taught English at Fulford Comprehensive School in the 1980s. I don't think either of us was very keen on it – I certainly gave up as soon as I could. What a small world!*
>
> *Brigid*

People are naturally inclined to believe that ours is an orderly world, governed by constant, predictable rules. However, life can be more bizarre than we are often willing to accept. During my journey I was witness to an incredible number of miracles. The fact that William's niece and James's first cousin had worked together for years in the same school was one more on the list. How many times did they talk or greet each other in the corridors, or in the school car park, without being aware that their relatives had died on the same rope on the slopes of a mountain in Switzerland many years earlier? How many times did they have a cup of tea together in the staff room without knowing that their pasts were so tragically connected? This notion is so extraordinary that had this book been fiction this last coincidence would, understandably, have been catalogued as an artificially contrived twist. However, it was real – it really happened that way.

Once recovered from the surprise, I turned my attention to Brigid's first email – to Epsom College, in Surrey, and the years that the Bell brothers spent there before the war, fighting each other, playing with each other, ignoring each other, or supporting each other, as most brothers do, usually all at the same time. I also read Brigid's warm account of her father's later life. In many ways, it looked like the kind of existence that his brother William might have eventually enjoyed, had he not died on the Matterhorn. Yes, it was easy to envisage William having his own family and children, a good professional career, and a comfortable social and economic position. Above all, it was easy to imagine William never giving up his dreams – neither literary nor mountaineering.

In the following days, Brigid and I exchanged plenty of emails. I sent her most of the documents that I had gathered and in return she kindly sent me the scans of William's diaries of 1947 and 1948, as well as several letters written by him, or received by the family after his death. In one of them, Heathcote W. Garrod, a don at Merton and a good friend of William, described him as 'one of the best and kindest of my friends,' and someone from whom he 'expected great things one day.' He also talked about one of William's poems, *Elegy I*, which Garrod defined as 'the best poem I know of the last five-and-twenty years.'

> *This summer the alarm is*
>
> *for every proud and passionate heart the same*
>
> *amid the ruin of our fleet and armies*

or where the unconqueror, conquered, falls in flame.

Wherever now a solitary defender

is squandering his breath,

in mourning or in death

wherever love has plotted our surrender.

Among all the documents that Brigid shared with me, the ones that I treasure the most are a series of pictures from her grandmother's photo album. They included some wonderful images of William's childhood, during a family vacation in Northern Ireland, from where the Bell family originated. In them, William appears as a happy-go-lucky teenager – not as the climber, or the poet, or the Oxford student, or the soldier that he would become someday. The caption says 'Portnablagh', a small village on the north-west coast of County Donegal, in Ireland, dated 1939, the last summer before the beginning of the war and the world went completely crazy. In the first of the pictures, William is in his swimming trunks, playing animatedly with his brother Robert and his father Harry. The second picture shows a group of eleven boys and girls of all ages, most of them in bathing suits. William is in the top row, naughtily smiling to the camera – his smile is unmistakable; I'd recognise it among a million others. The third image shows William, running frantically towards the water with other boys.

However, the most important pictures are of William's climbing holidays in the Alps in 1947 and 1948. Their value is extraordinary because, in some cases, they complement the information provided by Donald about the 1948 expedition, while in others they offer new details about William's climbing credentials. Above all, the images taken in 1947 offer a wonderful portrait of his relationship with Ian.

I had already seen one of the pictures – it was the same one that

Donald had shown me a couple of weeks earlier in Edinburgh, that had impressed me so profoundly: the one taken in Zermatt the day before the accident, with all the boys looking confidently to the camera, smiling, full of life. Two of the other pictures were taken in Orsières, Switzerland, at the train station, against a background of wooden goods wagons. All the members of the OUMC expedition are there, at platform three, posing together for the last time. They had arrived from Courmayeur, in Italy, on July 15. Their morale was low, as it had snowed copiously for the last three days and they had been forced to spend most of their time inside the huts, 'sewing buttons, and repairing gloves.'

According to Donald's notes, the sewing chief instructor was James, who probably acquired these skills during his time in the army. The boys had also tried to go from Courmayeur to Aosta but a general strike in Italy prevented them from taking the bus. It was the combination of bad weather in the Mont Blanc massif and the difficult political conditions in Italy that convinced them to return to Switzerland, via Val Ferret, and try their luck doing some climbs in the Zermatt area.

In Orsières, two members of the group, Jim Holt and Ronnie Briggs, decided to return to England. Perhaps for that reason there are no happy, smiling faces in those pictures. On the contrary, all the boys look tired and absent. William is again at the centre of the group, leaning on his ice axe, but he is looking down on both occasions as if he had not noticed that the camera was ready to immortalise the moment. To his right, Ian is staring directly at us with a half-smile, while James, holding some papers in his hands, has a composed, focused pose. In sharp contrast, the last picture of this lot is certainly a more relaxed one. It was taken in Zermatt, outside what seems to be a hotel or a restaurant. The hand-written caption below says 'the morning of July 24th 1948, before leaving for Matterhorn', and the boys are sitting around a table with drinks, chatting quite animatedly, it seems. As Donald

Right: In Donegal, 1939, the summer before war broke out. William and Robert Bell, with their father Harry Bell.

Right: William and Ian, alongside Colin Lindsay and guide Emil Kronig, on the summit of the Matterhorn in 1947 – the year before the accident.

Above: William and Ian, accompanied by Donald McKean and Colin Lindsay in Switzerland, July 1947.

Below: William Bell during the summer of 1947.

had told me, they had done some good climbs in the area in the preceding days and morale was very high again.

The other set of pictures were of the summer of 1947. One of them was taken on the summit of the Matterhorn. William and Ian are accompanied by their friend Colin Lindsay and two local guides. In the images, William wears a long coat and his face is covered with a scarf, as if he was in the middle of a sand storm in the desert. Standing next to him, Ian protects his eyes using enormous, rounded goggles, like a racing driver or a flying ace from World War I. He also wears what appears to be a big coat. By contrast, Emil Kronig, one of the local guides, is casually dressed, as if he were just taking a stroll in the park on a sunny Sunday afternoon rather than climbing a peak that barely seventy-five years earlier was every mountaineer's dream and nightmare. This picture confirmed what Heath-Stubbs had written in his introduction to *Mountains Beneath the Horizon*: that William and Ian had indeed climbed the Matterhorn together in 1947.

Of the two other pictures taken in 1947, one of them shows William standing alone on the gentle slope of a hillside, again his face covered as if he were a Bedouin. Behind him, an unidentified snowy peak dominates the valley. In the other photograph, taken on 23 July 1947, we can see William and Ian together again, but this time they are accompanied by Donald McKean and Colin Lindsay as well. They seem to be on some kind of promontory, with a deep valley running behind them. The caption does not specify the location but I am almost certain that the picture was taken not very far from Schwarzsee, a scenic place with a turquoise lake on the way from Zermatt to the Hörnli hut, which stands just a few yards away from the ridge leading to the summit.

All of these pictures showed that William and Ian were experienced climbers. In 1947, William had spent most of July in Arolla, climbing with other members of the OUMC before moving to

Zermatt, via the Haute Route, as the documents and letters acquired by Merton showed. Donald confirmed to me that his brother also spent the summer of 1947 climbing in the Alps, part of it with the OUMC group, and the rest with his family in Zermatt. So, by the time they started climbing the Matterhorn that morning of July 25 1948, Ian and William had already spent two full climbing seasons in the Alps, in addition to numerous other climbs in the Lake District, the Highlands and Snowdonia. By no means were they some foolish tenderfoots who, hypnotised by the beauty of the mountain, had recklessly decided to give it a try, totally unaware of what awaited them on its steep, treacherous slopes.

More importantly, the pictures confirmed that Ian and William not only knew each other quite well but they also trusted each other – otherwise they would not have carried out so many climbs together. This detail is noteworthy because trust is the only non-negotiable element when you choose a climbing partner – physical conditions or technical skills do matter but trust is even more important because of the fact that you are going to put your life in your partner's hands and vice versa. William and Ian, the High Church Tory of eighteenth century vintage and the Nonconformist, ardent Socialist, as James described them, might have very different political and social ideas. Their characters might also be completely opposite in many ways as well. Yet, they were more than friends; in some respects they were even more than brothers. They were comrades. Like soldiers on a battlefield, Ian and William were united by the unique bond that only those who confront death, relying on those standing beside them, come to experience and understand.

Needless to say, I gave Brigid the contact details of both Donald McKean and David Ogilvie in case she wanted to get in touch with them. To my delight, she told me a few days later that she had received 'a very nice reply from Donald', after she sent him a couple of pictures.

★

A couple of weeks before Christmas we sent Hillary Ogilvie the scarf that we had bought for her – the one like Marian's, which she had liked so much during our visit to Bloomfield. A few days later, we received a beautiful card from her accompanied by the following note:

> *Dear Marian and Mateo,*
>
> *The scarf is wonderful! Thank you very much for such a generous present. It has come at just the right time. The weather has been bitterly cold with snow, frost and freezing rain. No problem, my scarf keeps them at bay.*
>
> *With greetings and good wishes from us both*
>
> *Hillary*

I keep the note as if it were a precious treasure.

However, it was not all good news during these months. The moment I started reading Ian's diaries I realised that his 'obscure hand-writing', as his brother Donald had defined it, was in fact much more impenetrable than I had expected. Some scattered words, even small sentences in very rare cases, could be read here and there, showing that Ian not only was a good observer of the reality around him but that he also possessed a very compassionate character. However, the majority of the text was completely illegible. I recall the days I spent trying to decipher them, trying to make any sense out of them, as probably the most frustrating period during the entire journey. It felt like I was so close to Ian, and yet so distant at the same time, as if we were standing on the opposite banks of a fast-flowing river with no bridge between us. I sent samples of the diaries to several companies that specialised in transcribing old manuscripts, in the hope that they could read them. Unfortunately, all of them responded that it was an impossible job.

Early in March I received a fat letter with the thirteen red and white stars of the Valais flag on the envelope. It was sent by Joël Lonfant, the chief librarian of the Education, Culture and Sport Department of the Canton of Valais, one of the twenty-six cantons that form the Federal Republic of Switzerland, where Zermatt is located. I had contacted Joël several months earlier to request information about the accident. Now, together with a brief note, he had sent photocopies of every Swiss newspaper that, back in 1948, had published any news about the accident. These included the *Journal de Geneve*, the *Nouvelliste Valaisan*, the *Gazette de Lausanne*, the *Journal et Feuille d'Avis du Valais*, the *Journal de Sierre et du Valais Central*, *Le Rhone*, the *Walliser Bote*, the *Walliser Volksfreund* and the *Walliser Nachrichten*. However, none of them shed any new light on what had happened on the Matterhorn. In fact, most of them contained important mistakes and contradictions and it was evident that in some cases they had published the news without attempting to check the veracity of the facts that they were describing. For example, the *Journal de Geneve* described William, Ian and James as experienced climbers, while the *Walliser Volksfreund* speculated that their lack of familiarity with the Matterhorn could be the main factor behind the accident. Two of the German-speaking newspapers even said that it was William's brother, instead of Ian's, who decided to stay in the hut. Most of the newspapers even got Ian's name wrong – they called him Jan and one of them even changed the surname from McKean to Makken. After reading this, I was not at all surprised that in the days following the accident Donald McKean had been angry with the journalists and newspapers that covered the accident because of their lack of rigour.

★

On a sunny afternoon late in April, I had an amazing telephone conversation with Mrs Violet Cruickshank, the sister of James Napier, the boy rescued by William on the cliffs near Arbroath in 1946. When I contacted *The Arbroath Herald* to get information about the circumstances of the rescue they had asked me whether I would mind if they published an article about my search. 'Sure, of course', had been my carefree response, as I thought that they were just being nice and that nothing would actually be published. Honestly speaking, I didn't think that the newspaper, no matter how small it could be, would find my story interesting enough to dedicate any space to it. For that reason, when on a Sunday evening I received an email from someone called Karen Olivier, I didn't make the connection at all with the idea suggested by *The Herald's* journalist a couple of weeks earlier. The email said:

> *Dear Mr Cabello,*
>
> *I note with great interest your article in the Arbroath Herald entitled 'Author seeks cliff survivor from 1946'. It turns out this was my uncle James Napier. I am emailing on behalf of my mother Mrs Violet Cruickshank who is Mr Napier's sister. Unfortunately my uncle James died in 1995. My mother would be happy to relate to you what my uncle James went on to achieve in his life including a distinguished career in the British Army.*
>
> *Yours faithfully*
>
> *Karen Oliver*

Karen's email included her telephone number, so the next day I called her to check when it would be convenient for me to talk to her mother.

At 73, Mrs Cruickshank is a jovial, charming lady with an extraordinary memory. For me it was a delight talking to her about the day William saved her brother on the cliffs. She was seven at the time but still had vivid memories of it. "Eric – the boy who died – lived at number eighteen on our street, in Cairnie Loan, and we lived at number twenty-nine. His father was the manager of a grocery shop. He and my brother were friends and they went to the cliffs to try to find seagull eggs. My brother said that Eric went up too far; he told him not to climb any further but Eric didn't listen and he fell. He was killed."

She hadn't seen William but she remembered quite well how the police had visited their home and how her parents were extremely relieved that her brother was safe.

We also talked at length about the life that James came to enjoy after he was saved by William. According to her, it was a good, happy life. A life well lived, I recall were her words. James did his National Service in the army as a mechanic – 'although he was awarded a medal for being the best shooter in his platoon', she proudly added – a time that he deeply enjoyed. After a period stationed in Cyprus, he returned to England, where he got married. He lived in Newcastle until he died of cancer in 1995. He had four children, Violet said, all of whom were also married and themselves had children. James was a proud, warm grandfather who loved spending time playing with them.

We talked about many more things that afternoon – about post-war Arbroath, about her own life, and so on. It was a nice conversation. However, what stayed in my mind when I hung up was a sentence contained in the *Talmud*, the ancient codification of the Oral Law in Judaism, which says, 'Whoever saves a life, it is considered as if he saved an entire world.'

It is true. That day, back in 1946, William not only saved James's life but the lives of his four, still-to-be-born children as well, and the lives of the children of those children for generations to come.

17. A walk in the meadows of life

In the end, it is not the years in your life that count.
It is the life in your years.
Abraham Lincoln

I finished the first draft of the book at the end of May, less than twelve months after I had found William, Ian and James in Zermatt. The manuscript included the feedback, ideas and suggestions kindly provided by Donald McKean, David Ogilvie and Brigid Hamilton-Jones. For me it was important not only to know their opinion of the accuracy of the information in the book but also the overall approach I had used, the treatment given to the interviews, etc. Once more, their contributions were generous and substantial, and I am extremely grateful.

More or less at the same time, I finished reading Wade Davis's *Into the Silence*, the magnificent account of the British attempts to conquer Mount Everest in the aftermath of World War I. I had bought it a few months earlier but had deliberately decided not to touch until I had achieved some good progress with my own draft. Being a novice in the art of writing, I wanted to avoid being influenced, even if unconsciously, by what was celebrated by the public and critics alike as a great book.

Into the Silence does, indeed, make very interesting reading in many ways. However, the story that it tells has nothing to do with mine. In many respects they are completely opposite. Wade's is the epic account of the failed attempt to achieve what, at that time, seemed to be an impossible dream. The fight to reach the summit of Everest – a ruthless enemy – reflects the determination of Mallory and his companions to go beyond the limits of human endurance.

At stake was not only their own personal ambition but also the aspirations to grandeur of the British Empire. Victorious although completely prostrated after the war effort, Britain was trying to regain her international prestige. For that reason the entire book oozes with words such as honour, national pride, duty and glory.

In contrast, my story is much more modest. It revolves around small things like friendship and comradeship, everyday dreams and expectations, and the zest for life of three young students. William, Ian and James are no epic heroes. Nor did they aspire to be, even if, when forced by circumstances, they had to behave heroically at points in their lives. They were just anonymous, amateur climbers who attempted to climb the Matterhorn not because fame was waiting for them at the summit, but just for fun – for the pleasure that climbing gave them. They were neither exploring new routes nor trying to set any records. They did it because they were alive, and because staring at the beauty and serenity of the world from the top of mountains was their way to both celebrate and appreciate life. They were young, but not reckless or inexperienced – William and Ian in particular had a long history of successful climbs behind them. I am sure that they were totally aware of the risks that climbing involved as well – they knew what they were doing.

★

I have lost count of the number of climbing and mountaineering books that I have read since I started this journey. Yet, if I had to choose the most dramatic moment in any of them, it would be in *Annapurna*, when Maurice Herzog and his fellow climber Louis Lachenal, at the limit of their strength, decided to make a final push to reach the summit of the mountain on 3 June 1950. They were so exhausted that, in their words, it was possible to glimpse the certainty that they were heading to their own deaths. However, for them death was more desirable than failure: far more tolerable than returning to France without having achieved the goal of being the first to climb a 26,247-foot peak.

> *Now we were nearing our goal. In an hour or two a victory would be ours. Must we give up? No, that would be impossible. My whole being revolted against the idea. I had made up my mind irrevocably. Today we were consecrating an ideal, and no sacrifice was too great.*

Some may see this behaviour as borderline suicidal. The same attitude can be often found in Mallory's fixation with Everest. They would conquer the mountain or perish in the attempt. The day before making what would be his last effort to reach the top of the world, he wrote to his friend David Pye:

> *We are on the point of moving up again and the adventure looks more desperate than ever.*

Yet, up they went, cheerful to do it.

The case of William, Ian and James is completely different. That summer of 1948 their appetite for mountains had already been well satiated. They had spent several weeks scrambling in the Alps, climbing here and there: in the Mont Blanc massif, in Trient, in the Matter valley. They climbed the Tour Noir, the Aiguille du Nord, and Monte Rosa, among others. The Matterhorn was just the cherry on the top of the cake. No more than that – definitely not a matter of life or death.

William, Ian and James were not Mallory or Herzog. Yes, mountains were their passion but not their entire life, and certainly not something to die for. Their existence did not revolve exclusively around climbing. Mountains were indeed a source of joy for them, but so was, in the case of Ian, the defence of his political ideals; or his incipient career as a poet in the case of William; or music for James. They had so many things to live for back in Oxford and England; above anything else, their whole future and all the promises it brought with it was splendidly waiting for them.

Into the Wild, by the climber and author Jon Krakauer, explores the thirst for adventure of a young American university graduate, Chris McCandless, who embarked on a journey that would eventually lead him to suffer a slow and terrible death, completely alone in the Alaskan wilderness. In an attempt to understand McCandless's motives and the reasons behind his decisions, Krakauer recalls his own experience, fifteen years earlier, when he soloed the Devil's Thumb, a very difficult climb:

> *At that stage of my youth, death remained as abstract a concept as non-Euclidean geometry or marriage. I didn't yet appreciate its terrible finality or the havoc that it would wreak on those who'd entrusted the deceased with their hearts. I was stirred by the dark mystery of mortality. I couldn't resist stealing up to the edge of doom and peering over the brink.*

For William, Ian and James death was neither an abstract notion nor something that belonged exclusively to a distant future. No, for them death was something very real. The war had taught them that. In the case of William, his almost-fatal accident in Snowdonia, as well as the death of the boy MacDonald in front of him on the Arbroath cliffs two years earlier, were powerful reminders of the fragility of human life; 1948 was definitely a time to live, not to die while pursuing any sort of chimera in the mountains.

★

Since I first saw the tombstone of William, Ian and James in the Mountaineers' Cemetery, I have asked myself many times whether another reader would feel the same fascination for them that I do. This is an essential question because storytelling is a two-way form of communication, a sort of give-and-take with your potential readers. John Cheever, the American writer, said once that he couldn't write without thinking of them. In a stroke of genius he equated writing to kissing – something, he said, that you couldn't do alone. Obviously, after spending so much time in the company of William, Ian and James during this journey, it is difficult for me to be objective about them. However, looking back I think that there are two elements in their story that anybody may find appealing.

One is the fact that they had belonged to an extraordinary generation of British men and women who were willing to make the ultimate sacrifice for their country: a generation united by a war against evil and tyranny and who, once the war was over, stayed united while putting together the foundations of the nation as we know it today. This sense of togetherness is what caught my attention in Zermatt.

In time I came to understand that they were not just nice words written in bronze – William, the conservative Anglican; Ian, the non-conformist socialist, and James, the trooper who had once refused to become an officer, were true friends, despite all their differences. They were united in life in the same way that they have remained united in death. What brought them together when they were alive was much more important than whatever separated them. One of the things they had in common was their love for Britain. "They were patriots," their relatives told me. I believe them completely.

They died during an Olympic summer, four days before the beginning of the Austerity Games of 1948 in London. When I met them, the eyes of the world were fixed on London again. The opening ceremony of the XXX Olympiad was, with a celebration of the NHS as centrepiece, a tribute to the achievements of the post-war generation – William, Ian and James's generation. Had they returned safely from the Matterhorn that day, I am sure that each of them would have contributed to make Britain an even better country.

The other appealing factor is that their story is, somehow, everybody's story; their tragedy is everybody's tragedy as well. Paul Bowles, the author of *The Sheltering Sky*, once wrote that:

> *Because we don't know when we will die, we get to think of life as an inexhaustible well. Yet everything happens only a certain number of times and a very small number really. How many more times will you remember a certain afternoon of your childhood, an afternoon that is so deeply a part of your being that you can't even conceive of your life without it? Perhaps four, five times more, perhaps not even that. How many more times will you watch the full moon rise? Perhaps twenty. And yet it all seems limitless.*

We all die – we know it, but we also forget it quite easily. It is only when we are confronted with something as unnatural as the death of young people that we come to reflect on our own mortality. That happened to me in front of that tombstone in Zermatt. While writing this book, and after having the fright of my pulmonary embolism in Mozambique, I found myself wondering one morning what I would do if I knew that I only had one day, one week, or one month left to live. Most of us cannot choose how we die, but we can certainly choose how to live.

The most important lesson in the story of William, Ian and James is not how they died but instead how they chose to live. After reading their diaries, and the letters that they sent to their loved ones, and listening to the people who knew and cared for them, I can only conclude that they decided to live in a positive, life-affirming way: without fear or looking backward, only forward. They didn't wait for good things to happen to them – they tried hard to make them happen; they saw opportunities and seized them, whether it be a trip to the Alps, no matter how penniless they were, or a social gathering with good friends on a Sunday afternoon in Oxford. They certainly knew that life was fragile and finite and for that reason they treated it as a precious gift. They lived their lives to the fullest. Interestingly, they accomplished that because of their high level of awareness, and because of their depth of thinking, which is reflected in each of their writings. They knew how to make even the most everyday things extraordinary – the flight of a bird, a good book, a nice sunset. Finding this out was refreshing. I am glad to know that they made their short lives worth living.

★

Looking back I have realised that the seminal question of this book, the one that took me to the Mountaineers' Cemetery in the first place, (why people climb mountains) remains mostly unanswered. Perhaps that question simply has no answer for those who do not know the answer already.

In the initial chapter of *High Adventure*, Sir Edmund Hillary explains how, at the age of 20, he decided to start his climbing career during a trip to the South Island in New Zealand:

> *As I sat in the lounge that evening, the hum of voices suddenly hushed, and I looked up to see two young men coming into the room. They were fit and tanned; they had an unmistakable air of competence about them. I could hear a whisper going around the room: 'they have just climbed Mount Cook'. And soon they were the centre of an admiring group. I retreated to a corner of the lounge filled with a sense of futility at the dull, mundane nature of my existence. Those chaps, now, were really getting a bit of excitement out of life. I decided there and then to take up mountaineering. Tomorrow I'd climb something!*

For the most famous climber in history, for the conqueror of Everest, there was neither a heroic call from the heights nor a sublime perception of what awaited him beyond the clouds – it all began with the natural aspiration of every teenager in the world of trying to be cool. For Felice Benuzzi, climbing was a way to find his own self, temporarily lost among the crowds that filled the concentration camp near Mount Kenya. For Mallory, it was honour and pride that took him again and again to Mount Everest. For Boukreev, the reasons to climb mountains were almost mystical – in his own words, they were the temples of his religion. For Krakauer, looking into the abyss on the other side of the mountain was as important as the mountain itself. For my young friend Tom Codrington, the charm of mountains lies in the unresolved problems that they present.

However, if I had to choose a reason that in my opinion encapsulates why people climb mountains, I would pick what the Polish climber Robert Szymczak usually replies when, after someone dies on a mountain, he is asked why climbers keep going back:

It is not true that we go there to die. We go there to live.

During my journey, I have learnt that, for those seduced by the siren calls coming from the heights, their existence cannot be understood without climbing. 'Climbing is not a symbol or poetic metaphor of life – it is life itself,' writes Jan Alfred Szczepański, a Polish journalist and climber. The American Steve House, regarded as one of the greatest living climbers, simply 'lives to climb'. Period. Climbing is what makes them alive; it is the drug that has the virtue of transforming what are often shy, introspective people, of the kind that would normally go completely unnoticed in the middle of a crowd, into giants. Climbing floods them with passion – the feverish, child-like, contagious kind; it is what brings fire into their eyes. I know it because I have seen that bright, elusive flame in the people I talked to.

Yes, climbing is a disease. Climbers return again and again to mountains because they make them feel alive in a way that nothing else in the world can; in a way that those who, like me, have never experienced the exposure to this 'sickness' cannot understand. Most of us are rarely tested – really tested – throughout our lives. In most cases, our existence involves a lot of routine, repetitive processes within relatively safe, sanitary environments. Ask people and most of them will tell you that they never had to make a really big decision in their entire life, they just go with the flow and do whatever is expected of them on every occasion.

On the contrary, for those up on a mountain, every single choice can make the difference between living and dying. They are tested every single minute, and with every step they take. Often there are no second chances, no safety net. No wonder that for them, life back in the valley is absolutely dull. Some of them even talk about the 'horrors of paying bills' once they are back; others find the company of their spouses and children difficult for a few weeks, and others simply start planning their next trip the day after getting home.

Climbers and mountaineers go to mountains in the hope of measuring themselves against the most powerful rivals that nature may offer. And they do it, not despite the risks that it involves, but because the risks are an inherent part of the joy of being measured.

★

In May 2013, before dying in the Western Cwm at the foot of the Lhotse face of Everest, Alexey Bolotov said in an interview that 'a mountain in itself, is meaningless; they are nothing but a mix of ice and rocks. It is the human being who brings them to life, climbing them to the very top, and talking about them.'

So, perhaps looking for reasons why people climb mountains is a pointless exercise, one that could go on forever, because those reasons are as diverse as the human beings who actually climb them.

Or perhaps we should stop talking about reasons at all – all there is is an inexplicable craving, an uncontrollable passion that takes climbers beyond everything, including themselves. The rest, the explanations and the rationalisation of this desire, are just futile attempts to put into words something that belongs to the ethereal world of dreams, lusts and imagination. Something that certainly is almost impossible to describe. Something that I am unable to describe.

Epilogue

Charles S Houston, a member of the unsuccessful, and tragic, American expedition to K2 in 1953, wrote that climbing mountains represents 'a chance to be briefly free oneself of the small concerns of our common lives, to strip off nonessentials, to come down to the core of life itself. Food, shelter, and friends – these are the essentials, these plus faith and purpose and a deep and unrelenting determination.'

I love this vision of climbing as a form of liberation.

In many respects, writing this book was a liberating experience too: a way of abandoning my comfort zone and forcing myself to face some of my fears, as well as finding ways to overcome them. Already in my mid-forties, I will never go through the thrill of climbing a mountain like the Matterhorn, let alone peaks such as K2 or Annapurna. I will never endure the excruciating pain that is required to go beyond the threshold of my physical capacity in order to reach a distant, snowy summit. Writing this book, though, has been my Mount Everest, my winter ascent of Kanchenjunga, my north face of the Eiger, all in one. That's why I am so grateful to William, Ian and James – in a way, all this time they have been like loyal climbing partners to me. With their support, I have done things that I never thought I would ever experience. That's why this book is not only a detective story about them or about why people climb mountains – it is about my personal quest too.

Marian and I returned to Switzerland the following summer and for ten days we wandered along the mountain paths in the Bernese Oberland. Going to Zermatt was not initially part of that year's route but at some point the notion of being in the Alps and not visiting the Mountaineers' Cemetery to leave some flowers on William, Ian and James's tomb became unbearable. So we changed our plans and took a train to Zermatt.

Being there, in the cemetery, the most unexpected thing happened, though. I was not certain of how I was going to react, but I had always presumed that the re-encounter with the tombstone would be quite emotional. It was not. In a way, I even felt a certain sense of aloofness or detachment that I pointlessly tried to understand for the rest of the day.

The following morning we woke up quite early, as we wanted to cross to Italy via the Theodule Pass. The Matterhorn was with us all the way, majestic, and with it, the words of Gaston Rébuffat came to my mind:

> *You follow a track and you draw nearer; one step, then another, and your spirit, no less than your body, is in motion. You have just left the village, with its hustle and its insecurity, to cross a border, invisible but strongly felt, to penetrate a silence, to enter upon an intimacy. You stop, you listen, you sense a certain quality in things: the taste of the air, the sun enveloping the mountain, the undulation of the meadows, the camber of the moraine, and the curves of the glaciers. The other peaks are beautiful – the Matterhorn is a presence. You survey the way it divides the winds and rends the clouds; you question it. It reigns and governs. Its simple shape, its uncompromising ridges are the pre-conditions of its solitude: to live alone, if you want to preserve your integrity, you have to be doubly strong. The Matterhorn is protected by no other mountains. It is a law unto itself. It does not share the air it breathes.*

Then I finally understood.

I had spent an entire year looking for William, Ian and James – not about the circumstances of the accident or how they died but how they lived. I met their families, who talked about them as if they were still alive. I read their diaries, their poems, and their letters, full of dreams, of expectations and hopes, of laughs. They travelled with me to Mozambique, Mauritius and Bolivia. The four of us had spent long hours together in the departure lounges of many airports, in train stations, in impersonal hotels. For a year, they had been my loyal companions.

For that reason, the day before, on my return to the Mountaineers' Cemetery, I had been unable to make the connection between that vision I had of them and their cold tombstone. They were no longer just three names on a bronze plaque in a foreign graveyard. They are not dead to me. When I think about them, it is the photograph that Donald McKean gave me which comes to my mind: the picture taken when they arrived in Zermatt on 24 July 1948; a picture in which they glow, full of life.

This is the way I always see them: alive and smiling, even if their smiles are those of the day before.

Index

A

Anderegg, Melchior *30*
Annapurna *13, 18, 90, 192, 201*

B

Bates, Robert *13*
Bell, Brigid *174, 175*
Bell, Harry *115, 121, 173*
Bell, Mary Caroline *172, 173*
Bell, William *7, 14, 23, 25, 27, 28, 30, 38, 39, 41, 54, 68, 94, 99, 113, 141, 142, 145,*
      146, 149, 150, 151, 171, 177, 184
Benuzzi, Felice *13, 33, 198*
Binyon, Robert Laurence *15*
Bird, Sue *38, 39*
Blixen, Karen *123, 129*
Bolotov, Alexey *12, 91, 199*
Bonatti, Walter *13, 89, 96*
Boukreev, Anatoli *11*
Bourdillon, Tom *48*
Bowie, Don *90*
Bowles, Paul *196*
Braum, Herbert *22*
Bray, Libba *37*
Breithorn *15, 94, 121*
Briggs, Ronnie *182*
Broadbent, Steve *71, 73, 74, 77, 84*

C

Cambridge *17, 59, 94, 107, 110, 116, 161, 167*
Cambridge University Mountaineering Club *167*
Carnegie, Andrew *117*
Churchill, Winston *49, 81*
churchyard *7*
Codrington, Tom *74, 87, 93, 198*
Coffey, Maria *13, 52*
Colibasanu, Horia *90*
Conville, Jonathan *22*
Croz, Michel *17*

D

Davie, Ian *68, 121, 140, 172*
Davis, Wade *56, 191*
Dent Blanche *15*
Dickens, Charles *17*
Disney, Walt *87*
Dom *15*
Donne, John *153*
Douglas, Lord Francis *17*

E

Eiger *12, 13, 17, 31, 96, 201*
Elegies *41, 67*
Eliot, T.S *113*
Evans, Charles *48, 97*

R

Rébuffat, Gaston *18, 202*
Reid, Julian *59, 120*
Robert, Alain *93*
Ross, Andrew *31*
Royal Scots Greys *28, 29, 30*
Ruskin, John *16*

S

Schiller, Friedrich *73*
Seiler, Alexander *16*
Shakespeare, William *55*
Sharp, David *92*
Simpson, Joe *12, 13, 52, 92, 107, 108*
Simpson, Ted *141, 151*
Steck, Ueli *90*
Stephen, Leslie *13, 16*
Stevenson, Robert Louis *25*

T

Täschhorn *94*
Tour Rond *111*

U

Unsoeld, Willi *87*
Urubko, Denis *90, 91*

V

Venables, Stephen *7, 77, 78, 82, 179*
Viesturs, Ed *179*
Viney, Richard 'Dick' *48*

W

Weisshorn *7, 8, 15, 94, 142*
Whymper, Edward *13, 16*
Williams, Donald *22*
Wills, Alfred *15*
Woolf, Virginia *16*

Y

Young, Geoffrey *94*
Young, Geoffrey Winthrop *9*
Younghusband, Sir Francis *56*

Z

Zermatt *5, 7, 8, 11, 15, 16, 17, 18, 19, 20, 21, 22, 24, 25, 31, 32, 41, 43, 45, 50, 54, 61, 68, 72, 76, 79, 81, 101, 104, 120, 121, 130, 131, 140, 142, 149, 154, 168, 178, 179, 182, 185, 186, 188, 191, 195, 196, 201, 202, 203*
Zinalrothorn *15, 109*